Manhattan Review

Test Prep & Admissions ~~Consulting~~

Turbocharge Your SAT:
Writing & Language Test Guide

part of the 2nd Edition Series

April 20th, 2016

☐ *Designed as per the Revised SAT*

☐ *Complete & Challenging Training Sets:*
   10 Passages; 110 questions

☐ *Detailed explanations*

☐ *Comprehensive Grammar Review*

☐ *Detailed blueprint of Types of questions in*
   SAT-Writing & Language Test

☐ *Ample newly introduced Graphic questions*

www.manhattanreview.com

Copyright and Terms of Use

Copyright and Trademark

All materials herein (including names, terms, trademarks, designs, images, and graphics) are the property of Manhattan Review, except where otherwise noted. Except as permitted herein, no such material may be copied, reproduced, displayed or transmitted or otherwise used without the prior written permission of Manhattan Review. You are permitted to use material herein for your personal, noncommercial use, provided that you do not combine such material into a combination, collection, or compilation of material. If you have any questions regarding the use of the material, please contact Manhattan Review at info@manhattanreview.com.

This material may make reference to countries and persons. The use of such references is for hypothetical and demonstrative purposes only.

Terms of Use

By using this material, you acknowledge and agree to the terms of use contained herein.

No Warranties

This material is provided without warranty, either express or implied, including the implied warranties of merchantability, of fitness for a particular purpose and noninfringement. Manhattan Review does not warrant or make any representations regarding the use, accuracy or results of the use of this material. This material may make reference to other source materials. Manhattan Review is not responsible in any respect for the content of such other source materials, and disclaims all warranties and liabilities with respect to the other source materials.

Limitation on Liability

Manhattan Review shall not be responsible under any circumstances for any direct, indirect, special, punitive, or consequential damages ("Damages") that may arise from the use of this material. In addition, Manhattan Review does not guarantee the accuracy or completeness of its course materials, which are provided "as is" with no warranty, express or implied. Manhattan Review assumes no liability for any Damages from errors or omissions in the material, whether arising in contract, tort or otherwise.

SAT is a registered trademark of the College Board.
College Board does not endorse, nor is it affiliated in any way with, the owner of this product or any content herein.

10-Digit International Standard Book Number: (ISBN: 1-62926-099-1)
13-Digit International Standard Book Number: (ISBN: 978-1-62926-099-0)

Last updated on April 20th, 2016.

Manhattan Review, 275 Madison Avenue, Suite 1429, New York, NY 10016.
Phone: +1 (212) 316-2000. E-Mail: info@manhattanreview.com. Web: www.manhattanreview.com

About the Company

Manhattan Review's origin can be traced directly back to an Ivy League MBA classroom in 1999. While teaching advanced quantitative subjects to MBAs at Columbia Business School in New York City, Professor Dr. Joern Meissner developed a reputation for explaining complicated concepts in an understandable way. Prof. Meissner's students challenged him to assist their friends, who were frustrated with conventional test preparation options. In response, Prof. Meissner created original lectures that focused on presenting standardized test content in a simplified and intelligible manner, a method vastly different from the voluminous memorization and so-called tricks commonly offered by others. The new methodology immediately proved highly popular with students, inspiring the birth of Manhattan Review.

Since its founding, Manhattan Review has grown into a multi-national educational services firm, focusing on preparation for the major undergraduate and graduate admissions tests, college admissions consulting, and application advisory services, with thousands of highly satisfied students all over the world. Our SAT instruction is continuously expanded and updated by the Manhattan Review team, an enthusiastic group of master SAT professionals and senior academics. Our team ensures that Manhattan Review offers the most time-efficient and cost-effective preparation available for the SAT. Please visit www.ManhattanReview.com for further details.

About the Founder

Professor Dr. Joern Meissner has more than 25 years of teaching experience at the graduate and undergraduate levels. He is the founder of Manhattan Review, a worldwide leader in test prep services, and he created the original lectures for its first test preparation classes. Prof. Meissner is a graduate of Columbia Business School in New York City, where he received a PhD in Management Science. He has since served on the faculties of prestigious business schools in the United Kingdom and Germany. He is a recognized authority in the areas of supply chain management, logistics, and pricing strategy. Prof. Meissner thoroughly enjoys his research, but he believes that grasping an idea is only half of the fun. Conveying knowledge to others is even more fulfilling. This philosophy was crucial to the establishment of Manhattan Review, and remains its most cherished principle.

International Phone Numbers and Official Manhattan Review Websites

Manhattan Headquarters	+1-212-316-2000	www.manhattanreview.com
USA & Canada	+1-800-246-4600	www.manhattanreview.com
Argentina	+1-212-316-2000	www.review.com.ar
Australia	+61-3-9001-6618	www.manhattanreview.com
Austria	+43-720-115-549	www.review.at
Belgium	+32-2-808-5163	www.manhattanreview.be
Brazil	+1-212-316-2000	www.manhattanreview.com.br
Chile	+1-212-316-2000	www.manhattanreview.cl
China	+86-20-2910-1913	www.manhattanreview.cn
Czech Republic	+1-212-316-2000	www.review.cz
France	+33-1-8488-4204	www.review.fr
Germany	+49-89-3803-8856	www.review.de
Greece	+1-212-316-2000	www.review.com.gr
Hong Kong	+852-5808-2704	www.review.hk
Hungary	+1-212-316-2000	www.review.co.hu
India	+1-212-316-2000	www.review.in
Indonesia	+1-212-316-2000	www.manhattanreview.id
Ireland	+1-212-316-2000	www.gmat.ie
Italy	+39-06-9338-7617	www.manhattanreview.it
Japan	+81-3-4589-5125	www.manhattanreview.jp
Malaysia	+1-212-316-2000	www.review.my
Netherlands	+31-20-808-4399	www.manhattanreview.nl
New Zealand	+1-212-316-2000	www.review.co.nz
Philippines	+1-212-316-2000	www.review.ph
Poland	+1-212-316-2000	www.review.pl
Portugal	+1-212-316-2000	www.review.pt
Qatar	+1-212-316-2000	www.review.qa
Russia	+1-212-316-2000	www.manhattanreview.ru
Singapore	+65-3158-2571	www.gmat.sg
South Africa	+1-212-316-2000	www.manhattanreview.co.za
South Korea	+1-212-316-2000	www.manhattanreview.kr
Sweden	+1-212-316-2000	www.gmat.se
Spain	+34-911-876-504	www.review.es
Switzerland	+41-435-080-991	www.review.ch
Taiwan	+1-212-316-2000	www.gmat.tw
Thailand	+66-6-0003-5529	www.manhattanreview.com
Turkey	+1-212-316-2000	www.review.com.tr
United Arab Emirates	+1-212-316-2000	www.manhattanreview.ae
United Kingdom	+44-20-7060-9800	www.manhattanreview.co.uk
Rest of World	+1-212-316-2000	www.manhattanreview.com

Contents

Chapter 1

Welcome

Dear Students,

Here at Manhattan Review, we constantly strive to provide you the best educational content for standardized test preparation. We make a tremendous effort to keep making things better and better for you. This is especially important with respect to an examination such as the SAT. As you know that from Spring'16, SAT goes for a major change. The revised SAT is challenging now. A typical SAT aspirant is confused with so many available test-prep options . Your challenge is to choose a book or a tutor that prepares you for attaining your goal. We cannot say that we are one of the best, it is you who has to be the judge.

This book differs in many aspects from standard books available in the market. Unlike a book from any other prep company, our book discusses 9 SAT-like passages and 99 questions. Each question is explained in a detailed way. While discussing options, we explained each option keeping in mind why the correct option is right and why incorrect options are wrong. You will find sufficient number of questions on SAT's new introduction–Graphic based questions. The revised SAT-Writing & Language Test is more challenging than before. The passage itself may have a graph and an associated question. There would be at least a couple of graph based questions in the test. The book has as many as 5 graph-based passages, and associated questions.

In a nut shell, Manhattan Review's SAT-Writing & Language book is holistic and comprehensive in all respects; it is created so because we listen to what students need. Should you have any query, please feel to write to us at info@manhattanreview.com.

Happy Learning!

Professor Dr. Joern Meissner
& The Manhattan Review Team

Chapter 2

Introduction to the Revised SAT

The SAT has changed and the Revised SAT will take effect in the Spring of 2016. The revised SAT will comprise two major sections: one, Evidence-based Reading & Writing and two, Math. The essay, which now is optional is excluded from being a compulsory part of SAT Writing section. Evidence-based Reading & Writing has two sections: one, Reading (only Reading, no Critical word prefixed to it, but that does not mean that the new Reading Test will not test critical aspects of reading) and two, Writing & Language Test. This section has gone for a major change in its format. Questions testing your skills at writing, grammar, & language aspects will be taken up from a passage. With both Reading & Writing & Language sections being passage-based, they may also include info-graphics within the passages, and there would be one or two questions based on a graph or a chart. You may have a flavor of some math in the Reading passages & the Writing passages.

While the format of the Math test remains unchanged, there are new additions in Math section. It will focus more on Algebra and Data Analysis. You will see more questions on real-life situational charts and graphs in the test. There is an addition of two new topics: Trigonometry & Complex Numbers. There would be one or two questions testing your higher order thinking. Those questions may be in a set of two questions and would have a lengthy narration. Another special category of questions would be one in which you would be asked to interpret a situation described mathematically in word; there would be four options, each being at least two lines, and only one of the options is correct. Another change to the math section is that there would be a section of No-Calculator.

Two noticeable changes in the Revised SAT are: one, there is no negative marking and two, there would be only four options in MCQs.

Following table does a comparative analysis of The old SAT vs. The revised SAT.

The Old SAT vs. The Revised SAT

	Old SAT	Revised SAT

Sections	• Math
	• Critical Reading
	• Writing (incl. Essay)
		• Math
		• Evidence-based Reading & Writing
		  • Reading
		  • Writing & Language Test
		• Essay (optional; exclusive of Writing & Language test)

Content	• Reasoning Skills • Contextual vocabulary • Applied mathematical problems	• Reasoning Skills & knowledge of real-world situations • Evidence-based Reading, Writing, & Math problems • Introduction of graphs & charts in passages, thereby testing associated questions (even calculation-based questions) • Contextual vocabulary in broader contexts • Introduction of Trigonometry & Complex Numbers in math • Higher Order thinking questions in math
Question types	• Multiple Choice Questions (MCQ) • Student-produced response Questions (Grid-In) in math	• Multiple Choice Questions (MCQ) • Student-produced response Questions (Grid-In) in math
Number of options for MCQs	5 (A through E)	**4 (A through D)**

Negative marking	$-\frac{1}{4}$ for wrong answer	**No negative marking**
Scoring	<ul><li>Total score: 600–2400; incl. scores from Critical Reading, Writing, & Math (each score from 200–800)</li><li>Writing score includes Essay score</li></ul>	<ul><li>Total score: 400–1600; incl. scores from Evidence-based Reading and Writing, & Math (each scored from 200–800)</li><li>Essays are scored separately (1–4)</li><li>Sub-scores & Cross-scores (contribution from selected areas)</li></ul>
Timing	<ul><li>3 hours 45 minutes</li></ul>	<ul><li>3 hours (excluding essay)</li><li>3 hours 50 minutes (including essay)</li></ul>
Calculator access	Throughout the math section	There would be a No-Calculator section in the math section

Chapter 3

Introduction to SAT–Writing & Language Test

The SAT Writing & Language Test consists entirely of reading passages tested with the help of questions on those passages. Do not get confused SAT-Writing & Language passages with Reading Comprehension passages. Though SAT-Reading and SAT-Writing & Language passages look similar and have similar content, they have different format and test different aspects.

The SAT-Writing & Language Test questions will ask you to revise and edit text from a range of topics and content. Typical questions will ask you whether passages can be improved by making changes to words, phrases, tense, grammatical construction, punctuation, sentence structure, Comparison, parallelism, Idioms, modifications, sentence order, addition of a sentence, and deletion of a sentence.

Questions in this section will test your knowledge of grammar and of the elements of effective writing; they are embedded within the passage. Underlined word(s), phrase, or sentence that may or may not have error are marked with question numbers; you will be provided with four options to choose from in order to replace the underlined portion, and only one among them is grammatically correct and effectively conveys the desired contextual meaning. So, in a nut-shell, the passages will have many errors and your job is to make the passages error-free.

The SAT-Writing & Language Test is to be completed in 35 minutes, within which you have to answer a total of 44 questions across 4 individual passages. Each passage will be of 400 to 450 words and have 11 questions. Questions will be of many types, evaluating your general and specific understanding, revising and editing capability of content. Unlike five options per question as in the old SAT format, there would be only four options in the revised SAT.

•	Time	35 minutes
•	Number of questions	44
•	Number of passages	4
•	Length of a passage	400-450
•	Number of questions per passage	11
•	Number of options per question	4

3.1 Passage topics

The passage topics range from purely informational to Nonfictional narrative to reasoning-based. There will be one passage each on topics of careers, history & social studies, humanities, and science.

The passage from careers will present new trends, discussions, or debates in major fields of work, such as business, technology, and systems.

The passage from history and social studies will contain texts from anthropology, economics, sociology and psychology, geography, law or linguistics.

The passage from founding document and great global conversation will include content from documents important from historical perspective of the US or global level.

The passage on science can be on natural sciences, such as biology, geology, archaeology, chemistry, or physics.

3.2 The Writing & Language Test Scoring

This test will get an individual Test Score in the range of 10-40. It will also contribute towards the Evidence Based Reading and Writing score in the range of 200-800, along with the Writing Test. Select questions from this Test will be used to make two Cross-Test Scores, one Analysis in History/Social Studies and two, Analysis in Science, both in the range of 10-40. Two of the Sub Scores on SAT, 1-15, are also based on this section: Command of Evidence and Relevant Words in Context.

3.3 Types of questions

(1) **Writing part**

    (a) Expression of ideas

        i. Add a sentence (Placement type)

        Example:

        The writer wants to add the following sentence to the paragraph.

        <Recommended sentence>

        The best placement for the sentence is immediately

        A. before sentence 1
        B. before sentence 2
        C. after sentence 3
        D. after sentence 4

        ii. Add/Delete a sentence (Yes/No type)

        Example:

        The writer is considering deleting the underlined sentence. Should the writer do this?

        A. Yes, because it will strengthen the paragraph's focus...
        B. Yes, because it will strengthen the previous sentence's focus...
        C. No, because it will strengthen the paragraph's focus...
        D. No, because it will strengthen the previous sentence's focus...

    (b) Organizing ideas (Reordering of sentences)

        Example:

        Question: For the sake of cohesion of this passage, sentence 4 should be

        A. where it is now
        B. before sentence 2
        C. after sentence 3
        D. after sentence 4

(2) **Language part**

    (a) Subject-Verb agreement

(b) Pronoun referencing

(c) Adjective and Adverbs

(d) Verb/Tenses

(e) Punctuations (Comma, semi-colon, colon, period, dashes)

(f) Sentence Construction

    i. Fragment

    ii. Run-on sentence

(g) Joining two clauses

    i. Joining two independent clauses with semi-colon (;)

    ii. Joining an independent and a dependent clause with comma (,)

    iii. Joining two independent clauses with Coordinating Conjunctions FANBOYS (Comma + FANBOYS)

(h) Concision

(i) Modifications (mostly misplaced)

(j) Parallelism

(k) Comparisons

    i. Simple

    ii. Logical

(l) Idiomatic usage

(m) Usage of such, such as, like, as

(n) Usage of who, whom, whose, that, those, which, etc.

(o) Application of Quantity words

    i. Less/few

    ii. Lesser/fewer

    iii. Much/More/greater

    iv. A number of/Number of

(p) Diction

    i. Replacement with suitable word/phrase

    ii. Confusing words

        a. Accept/Except

        b. Allude/Elude

        c. Economic/Economical

(q) Conjunction pair

    i. Both. . . and

    ii. Either. . . or

    iii. Neither. . . nor

    iv. Not only. . . but also

    v. Between/among

(3) **Graphic part**

(a) Read data from a table/graph

(b) Relate data from a table/graph with text

This book provide you with 100 questions in 9 passages. You will get to know more about the question types when you attempt the questions.

Chapter 4

Grammar Review

4.1 Nouns

Nouns are used as subjects of sentences and as the objects of verbs and prepositions.

4.1.1 Common and Proper Nouns

Generally there are two types of nouns - common nouns and proper nouns.

· Common nouns refer to any place, person or thing, for example: girl, apartment, city.

· Proper nouns refer to particular places, persons and things, for example: Mark, New York, the White House.

4.1.2 Singular and Plural Nouns

Nouns can also be categorized as singular nouns and plural nouns. Sometimes certain nouns are used exclusively as either singular or plural nouns. That means they do not have a corresponding word in the other form.

· Singular nouns are used for a single occurrence, single person, single item, etc.

· Plural nouns are used for more than one occurrence, person, item, etc.

A quick comparison table of some tricky nouns in their singular and plural forms:

Singular form	Plural form
Alumnus	Alumni
Bacterium	Bacteria
Criterion	Criteria
Formula	Formulae
Medium	Media
Phenomenon	Phenomena

There are some singular nouns often mistaken as plural nouns because they end with "s".

Citrus

Economics

Glasses

Means

Measles

News

Physics

Scissors

Series

Species

Statistics

4.1.3 Countable and Uncountable Nouns

Another way to group nouns is by separating them into countable nouns and non-countable nouns. Countable nouns usually have both singular and plural forms. Uncountable nouns are used just as singular.

- Countable nouns can be counted by the numbers 1, 2, 3…Examples: desk, pen, person.

- Uncountable nouns cannot be counted in numbers. Rather, they are considered an entire item. Some commonly used uncountable nouns are: water, health, and money.

    Other examples of uncountable nouns include:

    Advice

    Anger

    Baggage

    Beauty

    Gasoline

    Information

    Luggage

    Smog

    Wheat

Sometimes a noun is used as an uncountable noun when it refers to the entire idea or substance, but it can be used as a countable noun when used in a context involving:

$\implies$ Countable pieces or containers for things.

   Uncountable: I prefer tea to coke.
   Countable: Two teas (two cups of tea) for us, please.

$\implies$ Different brands, makes, or types.

   Uncountable: I love cheese.
   Countable: There are so many cheeses to choose from.

$\implies$ A specific example.

   Uncountable: She has shiny hair.
   Countable: I found a hair today in my sandwich. How disgusting!

   Uncountable: He is great at sports.
   Countable: Skiing is a popular sport in Austria.

4.1.4 Collective Nouns

Certain nouns are used to describe a collection of people, items, or events in their entirety. Even though they are referring to more than one thing in the collection, they are singular.

However, when they are used to represent a number of collections, then they are plural.

Examples include:

Audience

Business

Choir

Committee

Company

Crowd

Family

Flock

Government

Group

Majority

Nation

Pack

Team

The Public

Unit

4.2 Pronouns

4.2.1 Pronoun Types

A pronoun is a part of speech that is typically used as a substitute for a noun or noun phrase. There are **eight subclasses** of pronouns, although some forms belong to more than one group:

(1) **personal pronouns** (I, you, he/she/it, we, you, they)

· Make sure sentences use them consistently.

(2) **possessive pronouns** (my/mine, his/her/its/hers, their/theirs, our/ours, etc.)

· Do not change the gender of a noun (as some languages, such as French, do).

(3) **reflexive pronouns** (myself, yourself, him/herself, ourselves, themselves, etc.)

· There are no reflexive verbs in English, as some languages have.

(4) **demonstrative pronouns** (this/these, that/those)

- These show nearness in location.
- Beware of the different between: that (pronoun) vs. that (conjunction)

(5) **reciprocal pronouns** (each other, one another)

(6) **interrogative pronouns** (who, what, when, where, why, etc.)

(7) **relative pronouns** (who, that, what, which, etc.)

- These relate different clauses in a sentence to each other.
- That vs. Which: restrictive vs. non-restrictive clauses
- Who vs. Whom: take subject vs. take object (Please see explanation later.)

(8) **indefinite pronouns** (any, none, somebody, nobody, anyone, etc.)

- none = singular (when it means "not one"); all = plural (if countable)
- much = can't be counted (use with uncountable nouns); many = can be counted (use with countable nouns)
- less = can't be counted (uncountable nouns); fewer = can be counted (countable nouns)

4.2.2 Nominative and Objective Cases

There are two pronominal cases: nominative (subject) and objective (object).

Subject: I, you, he/she/it, we, you, and they

Object: me, you, him/her/it, us, you, and them

Notice that the second person (both singular and plural) has only one form, *you*. The object case is used after verbs and prepositions:

We met *her* in a bookstore. She went to school with *us*.

Be careful of objects that consist of a proper noun (name) + a pronoun:

The puppy looked across the table at *Sarah* and *me*.

These situations can seem confusing, but there is an easy method to tell which pronoun (nominative or objective) is required. Just remove the other noun from the sentence to see if it still makes sense. If it does (as in "The puppy looked across the table at me"), then you have selected the correct pronoun; if it does not (as in "The puppy looked across the table at I"), then you should go back and check whether you selected the correct case for the pronoun (in this case it is the object of a preposition, *at*, so it should be in the objective case).

The relative pronoun *who* also has an objective case form, *whom*:

I kicked the girl *who* tried to steal my coat.

(I kicked the girl. *She* tried to steal my coat.)

I smiled at the girl *whom* I had kicked.

(I smiled at the girl. I had kicked *her*.)

4.2.3 Possessive Forms

All these pronouns have possessive forms that **do not** have apostrophes:

> my, your, his/her/its, our, your, their

These act as adjectives, and are followed by nouns. If there is no noun and the possessive form is used by itself, this form is said to be disjunctive:

> mine, yours, his/hers/its, ours, yours, theirs.

Again, there is no apostrophe. The relative pronoun *who* has the possessive form *whose*:

> I comforted the dog *whose* tail had been stepped on.

One is used as a supplementary pronoun; it **does** have an apostrophe in the possessive:

> *One* can only do *one's* best.

Note that *one's* is used only if the subject *one* is present; following with *his* would not be acceptable.

4.2.4 Agreement & Reference

There are several pronominal forms which seem to be plural but act as singular, taking singular verbs and singular pronouns if they act as antecedents. The most common of these words are *another, any, anybody, anything, each, either, every, everybody, neither, no one, nobody, none (not one)*, etc.; they must be followed by a singular verb, whatever the meaning might indicate:

> *Not one* of the bananas *was* ripe.
>
> *Everybody* wanted *his or her* own way.

Always look back to see what the pronoun refers to; where there is a generalization, it is sometimes tempting to treat a singular as a plural:

> *Man*, in all *his* glory, has ascended to the top of the food chain.

4.3 Adjectives

An adjective is a descriptive word which describes a noun, making it more specific:

> The *red* car
>
> The *old red* car
>
> The *large old red* car
>
> The two *young* professors lived in Greenwich Village.
>
> A *bright* light flashed through the window of the house.

Adjectives are usually arranged in order of specificity. Words normally used to perform other grammatical functions may be used as adjectives. These can be recognized by their position before the noun to which they apply:

remote-control car

war effort

Christmas cookies

spring carnival

Adjectives can also be used to form a **predicate** with the verb to *be*:

Chocolate *is yummy*.

Normally, only "true" adjectives can be used to form this kind of predicate. It is not possible to say:

Wrong: The cookies were *Christmas*.

Wrong: The carnival was *spring*.

In such cases, it is necessary to use the prop-word, *one*:

The cookies were *Christmas ones*.

There are three forms of a "true" adjective.

Normal:	big	beautiful
Comparative:	bigger	more beautiful
Superlative:	biggest	most beautiful

No agreement to a noun is necessary for an adjective.

Student Notes:

4.4   Adverbs

An adverb is a part of speech used mainly to modify verbs, but also adjectives and other adverbs. Adverbs describe how, where or when.

4.4.1   Adverbial Forms

Adverbs are formed in a few different ways.

Most adverbs are formed from adjectives by the addition of the ending *"-ly"* (as in suddenly, playfully, interestingly) or *"-ally"* after words in *-ic* (as in, automatically). Some adverbs are formed from nouns in combination with other suffixes: *-wise* (as in, clockwise, lengthwise) and *-ward(s)* (as in, northward, westward, skyward).

Some common adverbs have **no** suffixes, as in: *here/there, now, well, just.*

Some adverbs can describe other adverbs (the most common are intensifiers, such as "very", as in "very quick").

Some adverbs have the **same** form as their adjective counterparts, e.g., *fast, long, first.*

Not all words ending in -ly are adverbs: *lovely, ungainly,* and *likely* are adjectives. The word *only* and *early* may be either.

4.4.2   Adverbial Positions

Adverbs modify verbs in the same way adjectives qualify nouns.
The adverb **often follows the verb** it modifies:

> I shouted *loudly* to my friends across the theater.

Sometimes it precedes the verb:

> I *really* wanted to talk to her.

Sometimes position determines meaning:

> I think *clearly*. (My thinking is clear.)

> I *clearly* think. (It is clear that I think.)

Where emphasis is needed, the adverb may be put first, and the verb and subject inverted:

> *Never* have I seen such an ugly dog.

Student Notes:

4.5   Adverbs vs. Adjectives

4.5.1   Position and Meaning

When adverbs are used to modify adjectives, it is important to work out the relationships between them:

> She heard an *odd*, chilling sound.
>
> She heard an *oddly* chilling sound.

If one is not careful, it is easy to confuse whether a word is an adverb or an adjective, and, in either case, which other word it is modifying in the sentence.

The change from adjective to adverb can change the meaning drastically:

> The centaur appeared *quick*.
>
> The centaur appeared *quickly*.

In this example when the adjective is used, it appears that the centaur is quick, whereas when the adverb is used, it is the centaur's appearance which occurred quickly.

Good vs. well: Both *good* and *well* can be used as adjectives. When used as an adjective, *good* refers to morality or quality, and *well* refers to health. However, only *well* can be used as adverb and *good* is always an adjective.

Correct:

> I feel *good* about my work.
>
> I feel *well*.
>
> I am *well*.
>
> I'm doing *well*.

Wrong: I am doing *good*.

Note: This may feel like a correct sentence, as it is often used in colloquial English to express "how" are person is, but it is not grammatical in this instance.

Note also: "Good" can be a *noun* that refers to "good acts"

> I spend one day a month doing *good* for people in need.

4.5.2   Adverbs and Adjectives

Great care must be taken to align only with the word it actually modifies, because its positioning can affect the meaning of the sentence:

I ate some peas *only* yesterday - I don't need to eat any today.

I *only* ate some peas yesterday - I didn't do anything else.

I ate *only* some peas yesterday - I didn't eat anything else.

Only I ate some peas yesterday - Nobody else had any.

Early may be both adjective and adverb:

I take the *early* train.

I get up *early* to take the train.

4.5.3 Adjectives Only

Notice that some verbs may take adjectives to complete the meaning required (complementary adjectives). These verbs cannot form a complete thought without the required adjectives:

> He looks *confused* today.

> The music seemed *loud.*

Likely

Special care must be taken with the adjective **likely**. It is often mistaken for an adverb because of its form, but this is not an acceptable usage, for example:

> **Correct**: The Republic is *likely* to fall.

> **Wrong**: The Republic will likely fall.

Like (used as an adjective or preposition)

Like, with its opposite *unlike*, should be treated as an adjective or a preposition; that is, it must always have a noun to relate to. A predicate is formed with the verb *to be*:

> Life is *like* a box of chocolates. (Life resembles a box of chocolates.)

Used in the form of a phrase, *like* will link two nouns (or noun phrases) of the same kind. In this case, *like* functions as a preposition, a phrase-maker, and it is categorized so in some grammar books.

> *Like* any politician, he often told half-truths.

Like vs. Such As

In the above example, *like* is used to introduce similarity between two items or persons. This is an accepted usage on the SAT-W & L. In other words, *like* cannot be used to introduce examples or a subset of a category, which should used *such as*.

> **Correct**: I enjoy playing musical instruments *such as* the piano and violin.

> **Wrong**: I enjoy playing musical instruments *like* the piano and violin.

In sum, on the SAT-W & L, apply **like** before a noun or pronoun when emphasizing similar characteristics between two persons, groups or things. Use **such as** before a noun or phrase when introducing examples.

Like vs. As/As if/As though

Use *like* before a noun or pronoun.
Use *as* before a clause, adverb or prepositional phrase.
Use *as if* and *as though* before a clause.

Like is generally used as a preposition in such a context. *As* is generally used as an adverb while sometimes serving as a preposition with the meaning of "in the capacity of." As you can tell, the focus of the comparison shifts from the noun when used with *like* to the verb when used with *as, as if,* or *as though*.

> My mother's cheesecake tastes **like** glue.
>
> I love frozen pizza because there is no other snack **like** it.
>
> My mother's cheesecake tastes great, **as** a mother's cheesecake should.
>
> There are times, **as** now, that learning grammar becomes important.
>
> He golfed well again, **as** in the tournament last year.
>
> He served **as** captain in the navy.
>
> He often told half-truths, **as** any politician would.
>
> He acts **as if** he knows me.
>
> It looked **as if** a storm were on the way.
>
> He yelled at me **as though** it were my fault.

The same rule applies when you use the expressions *seem like* and *look like*.

> **Correct**:
> He *seemed like* a nice guy at first.
> That *looks like* a very tasty cake.
>
> **Wrong**: It *seemed like* he liked me.
> **Correct**: It *seemed as if* he liked me.

Here the comparison is with a clause, not a noun.

Due to

Due to is also used adjectivally, and must have a noun to attach itself to:

> My failure, *due to* a long-term illness during the semester, was disappointing.
>
> (That is, the failure was attributable to the long-term illness, not the disappointment, which would have had other causes, such as the failure.)

Owing to

If an adverbial link is needed, the expression *owing to* has lost its exclusively adjectival quality:

> My failure was disappointing *owing to* a long-term illness during the semester.
>
> (In this case, the disappointment at the failure was caused by the long-term illness during the semester.)

4.6   Prepositions

A preposition is a word that is placed before a noun making a particular relationship between it and the word to which it is attached.

4.6.1   Preposition Types

There are a few types of prepositions:

1) **Simple prepositions**: these are the most common prepositions, such as: *in, on, of, at, from, among, between, over, with, through, without.*

2) **Compound prepositions**: two prepositions used together as one, such as: *into, onto/on to (on to is British English, onto is American English), out of.*

3) **Complex prepositions**: a two- or three-word phrase that functions in the same way as a simple preposition, as in: *according to, as well as, except for, in favor of.*

Preposition, i.e. pre position – prepositions always occur before the thing they refer to.

In: I was born *in* that house. (Here that house is the object of the preposition *in*.)

Prepositional phrases may be adjectival or adverbial, according to what they modify:

   The girl *in my science class* kissed me.

Here, *in my science class* qualifies *girl*, and it is adjectival, but in:

   The girl kissed me *in my science class*.

in my science class modifies *kissed*, indicating where the kiss took place, and it is therefore adverbial.

Between refers to two things only; for more than two, use *among*.

   I sat *between* two very large people.

   We split the loot *among* the four of us.

4.6.2   Prepositions Frequently Misused

You should use prepositions carefully. Some prepositions are used interchangeably and carelessly.

For example:

beside vs. *besides*

   beside - at the side of someone or something

Frank stood *beside* Henry.

besides - in addition to

Besides his Swiss bank account, he has many others in Austria.

Exception: some idioms do not refer directly to either direct meaning.

She was beside herself with emotion.

The use of 'of' phrases such as: *could of, must of* are **incorrect** forms for *could have, must have*, etc.

between vs. *among*

Use the preposition *among* in situations involving more than two persons or things and use *between* in situations involving only two persons or things.

The money was divided *among* the workers.

The money was divided *between* the two boxers.

at vs. *with*:

Usually *at* for a thing but *with* for a person. Exceptions include: throw something *at* somebody *with* something, be angry *at* someone, be pleased *with* something, and others.

For example,

I went at Roger *with* a bat.

What's wrong with this sentence? Nothing actually, it is grammatically correct. It is simply an odd usage of the prepositions.

Be careful to use the right preposition for the meaning you want; *agree with* differs in meaning from *agree to, compare with* is distinct from *compare to*, and so on.

The expressions *superior to, preferable to* and *different from* are the only standard forms.

Student Notes:

4.6.3   Idioms with Prepositions

A

*a sequence **of***

*in accordance **with***

*be accused **of***

*acquiesce **in***

*access **to***

*adhere **to**, be an adherent **of** (follower)*

*affinity **with***

*be afraid **of***

*agree **with** (a person/idea)*

*agree **to** (a proposal or action)*

*aim **at***

*allow **for***

*an instance **of***

*analogy **with**, analogous **to***

*be attended **by** (not with)*

*attend **to***

*appeal **to** (a person)*

*approval **of***

*as a result **of***

*associate **with***

*attribute A **to** B (B is attributed to A)*

*authority **on***

B

*be based **on***

*have belief **in***

*be capable **of***

*be careful **of***

C

*be capable **of***

*care **about** - be considerate of; to think about*

care *for* - like

center *on*, center *upon* (not round)

collide *with* (not against)

comment *on*

compare *with*, in comparison *with* (used when emphasizing differences)

compare *to* (used when emphasizing similarities)

comply *with*

be composed *by* – be created by

be composed *of* – to be made up of

comprise *of*

be concerned *with*

concur *in* (an opinion)

concur *with* (a person)

conducive *to*

conform *to*

in conformity *with*

consist *of*

in contrast *to*

contrast A *with* B

credit *with* (not to)

give someone credit *for* (something or doing something)

D

in danger *of*

debate *on*, debate *over*

decide *on*

depend *on* (whether…, not if…), be dependent *on*, be independent *from*

determine *by*

differ *from* - to be unlike something; to be different from

differ *with* - to disagree with someone

discourage *from*

feel disgusted *with* (not at)

at one's disposal

distinguish *from*

be drawn *to*

E

be embarrassed **by** (not at)

end **with**, end **in** (not by)

be envious **of**, jealous **of**

be equal **to** (not as)

be essential **to**

except **for**, except that...

F

be familiar **with**

be fascinated **by**

H

be hindered **by**

I

be identical **with**, be identical **to**

be independent **from**

be indifferent **towards**

inherit **from**

instill something **in** someone (not instill someone with)

invest **in**

involve **in** (not by)

insist **on**, insist that someone do something

be isolated **from**

J

judge **by** (not on)

M

mistake **for**

N

native **to**

a native **of**

necessity **of**, *necessity* **for**

a need **for**

<u>O</u>

be oblivious **of**, *oblivious* **to**

<u>P</u>

participate **in**

preferable **to**

prevent someone **from** *doing something*

profit **by** *(not from)*

prohibit someone **from** *doing something*

protest **against** *(not at)*

<u>R</u>

receptive **of**, *receptive* **to**

be related **to**

relations **with** *(not towards)*

repent **of**

in response **to**

result **from**

result **in**

<u>S</u>

be in search **of** *(not for)*

be sensible **of**

be sensitive **to**

separate **from** *(not away from or out)*

similar **to**

be sparing **of** *(not with)*

be solicitous **of** *(not to)*

suffer **from** *(not with)*

*be superior **to***
*subscribe **to***
*sacrifice **for***

T

*tendency **to** (not for)*
*tinker **with** (not at, although this is British English usage)*
*be tolerant **of** (not to)*

W

*wait **for** - to spend time in waiting for someone or something*
*wait **on** – to serve someone, typically used in a restaurant setting*

4.7 Verbs

Verbs are a class of words that serve to indicate the occurrence or performance of an action, or the existence of a state or condition. English verbs, when discussed in grammar terms, are normally expressed in the infinitive form, together with "to". For example, to run, to walk, to work, etc.

4.7.1 Transitive and Intransitive Verbs

A verb is said to be **transitive** if it needs an object to complete the meaning:

Joern *kicked his brother.*

Whereas a verb is said to be **intransitive** if the meaning is complete in itself:

I *smiled.*

Leaves *fall.*

Some verbs may be either transitive or intransitive (meaning that they do not require an object to be complete, but they can take one to add detail):

I *ate.*

I *ate pudding.*

4.7.2 Active and Passive Voices

Transitive verbs may appear in **active** or **passive** constructions. In active verb constructions, the subject is directly concerned with the verbal process; it is the agent:

The hitman *killed* my boyfriend.

When an active construction is made passive, the object becomes the subject, and the relationship is reversed, so that the subject is now acted upon, and is thus 'passive':

My boyfriend *was killed* by the hitman.

4.7.3 Major Tenses

You will not have to memorize all of the commonly used tenses for the SAT-W & L, but a quick review of the tenses and their respective meanings will help you make sense of what can be a confusing topic.

Tense	Example
Simple Present (action frequently happening in the present)	He laughs. They laugh.
Perfect Progressive (action ongoing at this moment)	He is laughing. They are laughing.
Present Perfect (action started previously and completed thus far)	He has laughed. They have laughed.
Simple Past (completed action)	He laughed. They laughed.
Present Perfect Progressive (action started previously and ongoing at this moment)	He has been laughing. They have been laughing.
Past Perfect (action completed before another past time)	He had laughed. They had laughed.
Future (action to occur later)	He will laugh. They will laugh.
Future Progressive (action ongoing at a later time)	He will be laughing. They will be laughing.
Future Perfect (action regarded as completed at a later time)	He will have laughed. They will have laughed.
Future Perfect Progressive (action started at a later time and ongoing)	He will have been laughing. They will have been laughing.

A few Tense Examples

Present	Past	Past Participle
ring	rang	rung
walk	walked	walked

More examples

Present	Past	Future	Present Perfect	Past perfect	Future perfect	Present progressive	Conditional
dance	danced	will dance	has danced	had danced	will have danced	am danc-ing	would dance

Common Irregular Verbs

Infinitive Participle	Past Participle	Future Participle
do	did	done
go	went	gone
take	took	taken
rise	rose	risen
begin	began	begun
swim	swam	swum
throw	threw	thrown
break	broke	broken
burst	burst	burst
bring	brought	brought
lie	lay	lain
lay	laid	laid
get	got	got or gotten

An extensive list of irregular verbs can be found in Helpful Topics.

4.7.4   Moods: Indicative, Imperative and Subjunctive moods

Mood is a set of verb forms expressing a particular attitude. There are three main types of mood in English:

       ⟹ **Indicative**   ⟹ **Imperative**   ⟹ **Subjunctive**

The indicative mood is the most common one and it is used to express factual statements.

> I love playing the piano.

The imperative mood is used to express commands.

> Please close the window immediately!

The subjunctive mood expresses possibilities and wishes.

> If I were you, I would tell him my feelings.

The subjunctive is rarely used, but it is more often found in formal American usage than in British. The present subjunctive is very rare, having been overtaken by the present indicative, which it resembles in all parts except the third person singular: the subjunctive has no *-s* ending. The verb *to be*, however, has the form *be* for every person.

> I'll call you if need *be*.

The past subjunctive is identical with the ordinary past tense, but again, the verb *to be* is different, having the form *were* for all persons.

> If I *were* you, I would not do that.

Since the subjunctive expresses possibility, not fact, it is therefore found in:

(1) Clauses beginning with *if, as if, though, as though*, and

(2) After verbs expressing some kind of wish, recommendation, proposal, desire, regret, doubt, or demand.

The *if* (in subjunctive mood), *as if, though, as though* clauses express a condition that is NOT true.

Dependent Clause	,	Main Clause	Example
Present (True Condition)	,	Will/Can + Verb (base form)	**If you put your heart into it, you will be the winner.**
Past (Untrue Condition)	,	Would/Could + Verb (base form)	**If you put your heart into it, you could be the winner.**
Past Perfect (Untrue Condition)	,	Would have/Could have + Verb (past participle)	**If you had put your heart into it, you could have been the winner.**

When the subjective is used after verbs expressing some kind of wish, recommendation, proposal, desire, regret, doubt, or demand, there is a degree of uncertainty related to the final outcome.

Wrong

She recommended that John *should* take the ferry.

She recommended that John *takes* the ferry.

She recommended that John *had taken* the ferry.

Correct

She recommended that John *take* the ferry.

Note that you should ALWAYS just use the base form of the verb in such a subjunctive construction involving the *that* clause.

Regarding a list of words that are associated with the subjunctive mood, unfortunately, there's no hard and fast principle for it. This is what the linguists would call a lexical issue; the particular word and its meaning determine whether or not it can take an infinitive complement.

The following verbs can be used with a subjunctive that-clause:

advise

advocate

ask

beg

decide

decree

demand

desire

dictate

insist

intend

mandate

move (in the parliamentary sense)

order

petition

propose

recommend

request

require

resolve

suggest

urge

vote

Of these, the following can ALSO take an infinitive, X to Y construction:

advise

ask

beg

order

petition

request

require

urge

The infinitive group is to some degree distinguished by their being directed at a person, rather than at a state of affairs.

4.7.5   Participle

There are several parts of the verb system which function as if they were different parts of speech (in the case of a participle, an adjective). In grammar, the PARTICIPLE is the term for two verb forms, the PRESENT PARTICIPLE (the "-ing" participle) and the PAST PARTICIPLE (the "-ed" participle, also ending in "-d' and "-t"). Both participles may be used like adjectives, but only if the participle indicates some sort of permanent characteristic: "running water", "the missing link", "lost property".

The PRESENT PARTICIPLE ends in "-ing" and is used in combination with the auxiliary "be" for the progressive continuous, as in: "am driving", "has been talking", etc.

The PAST PARTICIPLE ends in "-ed", "-d" or "-t" for all regular verbs and many irregular verbs, but many irregular verbs end in "-en" and "-n" (as in, "stolen" and "known") or with a change in the middle vowel (as in, "sung").

4.7.5.1   Present Participle

The present participle ends in *-ing*. Like an adjective, it may be used to form a predicate with the verb *to be*:

> Her feelings for Bob *were burgeoning* quickly.
>
> She *is stunning* in that dress.

Used as an adjective, it holds the normal adjectival position:

> Her *burgeoning* feelings for Bob surprised her.
>
> The *stunning* woman looked straight at me.

Participles are commonly found in phrases alongside the main part of the sentence:

> *Burgeoning* rapidly, *her feelings* for Bob rose to an untenable level.

If there is no appropriate noun, the sentence becomes nonsensical. The falsely assigned participle is known as 'dangling' or 'misrelated':

> **Wrong:** *Burgeoning* rapidly, *she* was soon unable to control her feelings for Bob.

As we will discuss in the Writing & Language Test practice section, this is one of the most common errors on the SAT-W & L, so learn to recognize a misplaced modifier (dangling participle), and you will have great success with these questions.

4.7.5.2   Past Participle

The past participle ends in *-(e)d* or *-t* in most verbs. A few archaic forms remain; these are verbs which make the past tense by changing the internal vowel, e.g., *write, wrote; see, saw*. These have participles that end in *-(e)n*, e.g. *written, seen*. The past participle forms a compound tense (perfect) with the addition of the verb *to have*. This denotes the perfected or completed action:

> I have *decided* to leave you.

It is useful to be able to recognize tenses because another of the most common errors on the SAT-W & L is changing tenses needlessly in the middle of a sentence. Make sure that the answer you select does not have a change of tense which is not justified by the meaning of the sentence.

Used adjectivally, however, the past participle may also form a predicate with the verb *to be*.

I *have slain* you.

You *are slain*.

As with the present participle, the past participle must be related to its proper noun when forming a modifying phrase:

Embarrassed by her faux pas, *Ellen* left the room.

If the participle is misrelated (misplaced), comic results will occur:

Wrong: *Covered* with aluminum foil, I popped the lasagna into the oven.

(Here it is me, and not the lasagna, that is covered with aluminum foil!)

4.7.5.3   Special Situations

Absolute participle constructions are rare, and normally consist of a noun and participle - the noun to which the participle refers is actually present, although it does not have a function in the rest of the sentence:

The game being over, the players all went home.

Weather permitting, the wedding will be held outdoors.

A similar construction has the preposition *with*:

I returned to school *with my essay revised*.

A few participles have virtually become prepositions in their own right. These are:

barring, considering, excepting, including, owing (to), regarding, respecting, seeing, touching;

and the past forms,

excepted, provided, given.

Student Notes:

4.7.6   Gerunds & Infinitives

The GERUND is a verbal noun, ending in "-ing". Many grammarians of English use the term PARTICIPLE to include the gerund. Take the word "visiting" in the sentence: "They appreciate my visiting their parents regularly."

Like participles, gerunds are verbal elements which take on the role of another part of speech (in this case, that of a noun).

More common is the form ending in *-ing*, and this is identical with the form of the present participle. The two are distinguished only by function:

> Taking this route was a mistake. (subject, *taking*)
>
> Why are we going this way? (participle, *going*)

There is no preferred version, but it is important to maintain parallelism in your constructions.

If an ordinary noun can be substituted for the *-ing* form, then it is a gerund, e.g.,

> *Taking it* was the fun part.
>
> *Its capture* was the fun part.

The gerund retains its verbal function by taking an object:

> *Owning a monkey* is very unconventional.

Less commonly, the noun function dictates the form:

> *The wearing of pink* by red-headed people is a major fashion crime. (Wearing pink ...)

Where a noun or pronoun is used with a gerund, it should be in the possessive case:

> *My admonishing him* will not change his mind.
>
> It was *his winning* that bothered me, not *my losing*.
>
> I can't stand *my mother's telling* my friends embarrassing stories about me.

Any word may be used as an attributive (adjective) if placed before a noun. A gerund may be used this way (called a *gerundive*); its form is identical with the present participle, but the meaning will be different:

> A *building* reputation - participle (a reputation that is building)
>
> Some *building* blocks - gerund (blocks for building with)
>
> A *working* appliance - participle (an appliance that works)
>
> *working* papers - gerund (papers which allow you to work)

The infinitive form of a verb has the word "to" proceeding it:

> to + verb

The infinitive form may be used in this function:

> To err is human, to forgive, divine.
>
> (= Error is human; forgiveness is divine.)

Care must be taken not to use a mixture of the two forms:

Talking to him was one thing, but kissing him was entirely another!

To talk to him was one thing, but to kiss him was entirely another!

Not: Talking to him was one thing, but to kiss him was entirely another!

Do avoid inserting a word or a phrase between the "to" and the "verb" in the infinitive form. This error is known as a *split infinitive.*

<u>Wrong</u>

I asked him to quickly clean the table.

<u>Correct</u>

I asked him to clean the table quickly.

Student Notes:

4.8   Conjunctions

Conjunctions are used to connect words or constructions. You should simply keep in mind that the most common conjunctions are AND, BUT, OR, which are used to connect units (nouns, phrases, gerunds, and clauses) of equal status and function. The other conjunctions, BECAUSE, IF, ALTHOUGH, AS, connect a subordinate clause to its superordinate clause, as in "We did it BECAUSE he told us to."

In general, don't begin sentences with conjunctions - *however* is better than *but* for this, but *however* goes best after semicolons, or use the adverb *instead*.

Correlative expressions such as *either/or, neither/nor, both/and, not only/but also* and *not/but* should all correlate ideas expressed with the same grammatical construction.

Special care has to be taken with clauses: only clauses of the same kind can be joined with a conjunction. Similarly, a phrase cannot be joined to a clause.

American usage is extremely fastidious in making constructions parallel, and this is another one of the common tricks in the Sentence Correction questions. Keep a lookout for conjunctions and lists, and you will be able to catch these errors.

4.9   Transition words

The following table of signaling or trigger words may help you understand the tone, style, and the meaning of the passage.

Continuation of thoughts	Opposing thought	Conclusion
Moreover	However	Therefore
Furthermore	But	Hence
In addition	Despite	So
Secondly	In spite of	Implies
Similarly	On the contrary	As a result
Also	Nevertheless	Thus
Too	Conversely	In short
For example	Instead	Inferred
Since	Yet	Consequently
Because	Rather than	In other words
Evidently	Still	
For instance	Surprisingly	
Illustrated by	While	
And	Although	
Analogy	Though	
Analogous	On the other hand	
Considering similar experiences	Even if	
	Actually	
	Notwithstanding	

4.10 Helpful Topics

4.10.1 Punctuation

Punctuation is the practice in writing of using a set of marks to regulate text and clarify its meaning, mainly by separating or linking words, phrases, and clauses. Currently, punctuation is not used as heavily as in the past. Punctuation styles vary from individual, newspaper to newspaper, and press to press in terms of what they consider necessary.

Improper punctuation can create ambiguities or misunderstandings in writing, especially when the *comma* is misused. For example, consider the following examples:

"They did not go, because they were lazy."

In this case, the people in question did not go for one reason: "because they were lazy."

But consider the sentence again:

"They did not go because they were lazy."

In this case, without the comma, the people probably DID go, but not because they were lazy, and instead for some other reason (they did not go because they were lazy, they went because they were tired).

Periods and Commas

(1) **Periods and Commas**: These are the most common form of punctuation. The period ends a sentence, whereas the comma marks out associated words within sentences. Commas are used for pauses, prepositional phrases, and appositive clauses offset from the rest of the sentence to rename a proper noun (Thomas, a baker,). They are the rest stop in the English language.

(2) **Colons, Semicolons, and Dashes (or Hypens)**: Many people avoid the use of the colon and semicolon because of uncertainty as to their precise uses. In less formal writing, the dash is often used to take the place of both the colon and the semi-colon. The rule is that both colons and semicolons must follow a complete independent clause. A semicolon must be followed by another complete clause, either dependent or independent. A colon may be followed by a list or phrase, or by a complete clause.

   · The APOSTROPHE (') is used to show possession: Those books are Thomas's books.
   · The COLON (:) is normally used in a sentence to lead from one idea to its consequences or logical continuation. The colon is used to lead from one thought to another.
   · The SEMICOLON (;) is normally used to link two parallel statements.
   · Consider the following examples:
     – COLON: "There was no truth in the accusation: they rejected it utterly."

        * Points to a cause/effect relationship, as a result of...

   – SEMICOLON: "There was no truth in the accusation; it was totally false." (Here two parallel statements are linked - "no truth" and "totally false". In the COLON example, the consequence is stated after the insertion of the colon).

        * Re-states initial premise, creates relation between disparate parts

        * Technically these sentences could be broken down into two separate sentences and they would remain grammatically sound. Two sentences, however, would suggest separateness (which in speech the voice would convey with a longer pause) that might not always be appropriate.

· HYPHENS or DASHES: The hyphen, or dash, is perhaps most important in order to avoid ambiguity, and is used to link words. Consider the following example:

   – "Fifty-odd people" and "Fifty odd people". When the hyphen is used, the passage means "approximately fifty people", while the second passage means "fifty strange(odd) people".

Otherwise, the use of the hyphen is declining. It was formerly used to separate vowels (co-ordinate, make-up), but this practice is disappearing.

For example: House plant → house-plant → houseplant

4.10.2   List of Irregular Verbs

To correctly use the verbs in different tense forms, please study the list carefully.

Base Form	Past Tense	Past Participle
Awake	Awaked; awoke	Awaked; awoken
Be	Was/Were	Been
Beat	Beat	Beat; beaten
Become	Became	Become
Begin	Began	Begun
Bend	Bent	Bent
Bite	Bit	Bitten
Bleed	Bled	Bled
Blow	Blew	Blown
Break	Broke	Broken
Bring	Brought	Brought
Build	Built	Built
Burst	Burst	Burst
Buy	Bought	Bought
Catch	Caught	Caught
Choose	Chose	Chosen
Come	Came	Come
Cost	Cost	Cost
Cut	Cut	Cut
Deal	Dealt	Dealt
Dig	Dug	Dug
Dive	Dived; dove	Dived
Do	Did	Done
Draw	Drew	Drawn
Dream	Dreamed; dreamt	Dreamed; dreamt
Drink	Drank	Drunk
Drive	Drove	Driven
Eat	Ate	Eaten
Fall	Fell	Fallen
Feed	Fed	Fed
Feel	Felt	Felt
Fight	Fought	Fought
Find	Found	Found
Fit	Fitted; fit	Fitted; fit
Fly	Flew	Flown
Forget	Forgot	Forgotten
Freeze	Froze	Frozen
Get	Got	Gotten; got
Give	Gave	Given
Go	Went	Gone
Grow	Grew	Grown

Base Form	Past Tense	Past Participle
Hang (an object)	Hung	Hung
Hang (a person)	Hanged	Hanged
Hear	Heard	Heard
Hide	Hid	Hidden; hid
Hit	Hit	Hit
Hold	Held	Held
Hurt	Hurt	Hurt
Keep	Kept	Kept
Kneel	Knelt; kneeled	Knelt; kneeled
Knit	Knit; knitted	Knit; knitted
Know	Knew	Known
Lay (put down)	Laid	Laid
Lead	Led	Led
Lean	Leaned	Leaned
Leave	Left	Left
Lend	Lent	Lent
Let	Let	Let
Lie (recline)	Lay	Lain
Light	Lighted; lit	Lighted; lit
Lose	Lost	Lost
Make	Made	Made
Mean	Meant	Meant
Meet	Met	Met
Pay	Paid	Paid
Prove	Proved	Proved; proven
Put	Put	Put
Quit (leave a place uncommon in American English)	Quit; quitted	Quit; quitted
Quit (end a job)	Quit	Quit
Read	Read	Read
Rid	Rid	Rid; ridden
Ride	Rode	Ridden
Ring	Rang	Rung
Run	Ran	Run
Say	Said	Said
See	Saw	Seen
Sell	Sold	Sold
Send	Sent	Sent
Set	Set	Set
Shake	Shook	Shaken
Shine	Shone; shined (polish)	Shone; shined (polish)

Base Form	Past Tense	Past Participle
Shoot	Shot	Shot
Show	Showed	Showed; shown
Shrink	Shrank	Shrunk
Shut	Shut	Shut
Sit	Sat	Sat
Sleep	Slept	Slept
Slide	Slid	Slid
Speak	Spoke	Spoken
Speed	Sped; speeded	Sped; speeded
Spend	Spent	Spent
Spin	Spun	Spun
Spring	Sprang	Sprung
Stand	Stood	Stood
Steal	Stole	Stolen
Stick	Stuck	Stuck
Sting	Stung	Stung
Strike	Struck	Struck; strucken
Swear	Swore	Sworn
Swim	Swam	Swum
Swing	Swung	Swung
Take	Took	Taken
Teach	Taught	Taught
Tear	Tore	Torn
Tell	Told	Told
Think	Thought	Thought
Throw	Threw	Thrown
Wake	Waked; woke	Waked; woken
Wear	Wore	Worn
Win	Won	Won
Wring	Wrung	Wrung
Write	Wrote	Written

4.10.3   Words Frequently Confused

The following words are often misused, even by experienced writers:

accumulative, cumulative	affluent, effluent
adverse, averse	allusion, illusion, delusion alternate, alternative
affect, effect	amiable, amicable, amenable

anomaly, analogy

apposite, opposite

appraise, apprise
ascent, assent, accent

belated, elated

beneficent, benevolent

biannual, biennial

censer, censor, censure

colloquy, obloquy

complement, compliment

contemptuous, contemptible

continual, continuous, contiguous

credible, credulous

decry, descry

deduce, deduct

deficient, defective

denote, connote

deprecate, depreciate

dependent, dependant

derisive, derisory

devolve, evolve
digress, regress

disburse, disperse

discrete, discreet

disquisition, inquisition

economic, economical

edible, eatable

efficient, effectual, effective

eject, inject

elusive, illusive

erotic, exotic

erupt, disrupt

euphony, cacophony

fallacious, fallible

fictitious, factitious

further, farther

grouchy, grungy

historic, historical

hoard, horde
homogenous, homogeneous

human, humane

hypercritical, hypocritical

inchoate, chaotic

induce, indict

ineligible, illegible

ingenious, ingenuous

insidious, invidious

intermediate, intermediary

introspection, retrospection

judicial, judicious

lie, lay

lightening, lightning

luxurious, luxuriant

monitory, monetary

negligible, negligent

notable, notorious

observance, observation
obtrude, intrude

ordinance, ordnance

oral, aural

overt, covert

peaceful, peaceable

perspective, perceptive

perspicacious, perspicuous

precipitate, precipitous

precede, proceed

preclude, prelude

prescribe, proscribe

principle, principal

prospective, prosperous

raise, rise

reputed, imputed

resource, recourse

salutary, salubrious

seasonal, seasonable

spasmodic, sporadic

tacit, taciturn

temperature, temperament

temporize, extemporize

tortuous, torturous

uninterested, disinterested

urban, urbane

veracious, voracious

vocation, avocation

If you think you may not know the difference between any of these pairs, or would like to brush up on the meanings of any of these words, please ask your instructor to clarify them, or look them up in a dictionary before your test date.

Student Notes:

4.10.4   Standard vs. Non-standard Usage

There are many American expressions that do not meet standard requirements; most of these are easily recognized, but some may raise doubts. As a general rule, *kind of* and *sort of* are to be avoided altogether:

> I was *sort of* hurt by that.

If used adjectivally - and this would be possible - *kind of* does not have an article:

I thought I saw you with some *kind of* food.

The expression *those (these) kind of things* is particularily offensive, since *kind* and *sort* are singular and would properly be preceded by *that* or *this*. Similarly, the ending *-s* should never be attached to compounds of *-where*, e.g., *somewhere*. The *-s* ending is, however to be found in the compounds of *-ways*, e.g., *always, sideways, longways, lengthways*, but *anyways* and *ways* are nonstandard forms, as are *someway, noway* and *nohow*. Nonstandard also are the expressions *can't seem to*, for 'seem unable to' and *go to*, meaning 'intend'. *Any* should not be used adverbially:

Wrong: I don't think I hurt him *any*.

The correct expression is *at all*. I don't think I hurt him *at all*.

Adjectives should not be used as adverbs:

Wrong: We agreed on the specifics *some*; (use *some* for 'somewhat')

Wrong: I thought my plan would *sure* succeed; (use *sure* for 'surely', 'certainly'.)

Wrong: I noticed a guy who was *real* cute standing outside; (use *real* for 'really'.)

Non-standard usages would include verbs used as nouns, as in *eats* or *invite* (invitation), prepositions used in conjunctions, or *on account of* for 'because':

Wrong: I liked him *on account* he made me toys and things.

All should not be followed by *of* unless a pronoun follows:

I hate *all those people*.

I hate *all of you*!

Other nonstandard expressions include:

Nonstandard	**Standard**
be at	be
both alike	either 'both' or 'alike'
bring	take
equally near	equally
have a loan of	borrow
have got	have
human	human being
in back of	behind
inside of	within
lose out	lose
no account, no good	worthless
no place	nowhere
nowhere near	not nearly
off of	from or completely
out loud	aloud
outside of	outside or except
over with	over/ended
plenty, mighty	very

Student Notes:

Chapter 5

Practice Questions

5.1   Passage 1: Role of WTO

Passage 1

Role of WTO

Questions 1-11 are based on the following passage.

Environmental concern and development are inextricably linked. Experience demonstrates that environmental standards and cleaner production are compatible **1** <u>with</u> and supportive of economic growth. Healthy people and ecosystems are more productive. This link between economic growth and environmental improvement is enshrined, together with the commitment to development, in the World Trade Organization's Preamble, **2** <u>that</u> includes sustainable development as a basic objective of the trading system. In endorsing this concept, despite some reservations, WTO members unanimously recognized that trade and the **3** <u>economic growth the WTO helps to create must be fostered</u> in the context of sustainable development which integrates economic, social and environmental policies. **4** Economic growth, sustainable development, and opportunity for citizens are fundamental goals of every society.

5 <u>And the record</u> of the past five decades

1. **(A)** NO CHANGE
   (B) of
   (C) to
   (D) DELETE

2. **(A)** NO CHANGE
   (B) which
   (C) where
   (D) who

3. **(A)** NO CHANGE
   (B) economic growth that the WTO helps to create must be fostered
   (C) economic growth the WTO helps to create in must be fostered
   (D) economic growth that the WTO helps in creation of must be fostered

4. The author wants to add the following sentence. Should the author do so?

   On the contrary, the IMF's (International Monetary Fund) primary purpose is to ensure the stability of the international monetary system.

   (A) Yes, because role of the WTO should be viewed against the IMF.
   (B) Yes, because though the primary purpose of the IMF is to ensure the stability of the international monetary system, it would have its secondary purpose as sustainable development and environment protection.

clearly shows how the trading system has helped us reach some of these goals.

[1] Since 1960, the WTO has negotiated a 90% drop in tariffs, and non-tariff barriers to trade **6** has also been dramatically reduced. [2] Moreover, market access for agriculture and services will be further expanded **7** upon concluding the next Uruguay Round. [3] Thus, since 1960 trade has grown fifteen-fold; world economic production has quadrupled; and world per capita income has more than doubled. [4] However, has the World Trade Organization done enough to promote sustainable development and protect the environment? The answer is yet to be presented by the WTO. **8**

In reference to the concept of sustainable development, **9** the Brundtland Commission Report of 1987, "we must meet the needs of the present without compromising the ability of future generations to meet their own needs." Have any laws been made to make sustainable development mandatory? Taking into account state practice, treaty law, international case law and relevant legal literature, economists have found that **10** sustainable development is not yet a norm of international law. Currently it reflects a policy goal of the international community. This

(C) No, because reference of the IMF at this point is a distraction rather than a beneficial addition.

(D) No, because the placement of the placement of suggested sentence is at wrong place.

5. Which of the following CANNOT replace the underlined portion without compromising the meaning of the sentence?

  (A) NO CHANGE

  (B) The record

  (C) However, the record

  (D) Additionally, the record

6. **(A)** NO CHANGE

  (B) have

  (C) would have

  (D) Delete

7. **(A)** NO CHANGE

  (B) after the conclusion of

  (C) for the conclusion of

  (D) in the conclusion of

8. For the sake of cohesion of this paragraph, sentence 3 should be

  (A) where it is now

  (B) placed before sentence 1

  (C) placed after sentence 1

  (D) placed after sentence 4

9. **(A)** NO CHANGE

  (B) the Brundtland Commission Report of 1987

  (C) the Brundtland Commission Report of 1987:

  (D) the Brundtland Commission Report of 1987 stated,

10. **(A)** NO CHANGE

  (B) sustainable development are not

  (C) sustainable development and are not

method of taking a concept so important only as a precautionary guideline has brought the WTO's intentions regarding sustainable development into question.

(D) sustainable development is

11. **(A)** NO CHANGE
    (B) decreased on year to year (Y-O-Y) basis, so would the number against their counterparts.
    (C) increased on year to year (Y-O-Y) basis, so would the number, mostly against their counterparts, increase.
    (D) increased on year to year (Y-O-Y)

It is to be noted that number of complaints against the developed nations by the developing nations and vice-versa has been a roller-coaster ride (see the graph); from the beginning, whenever the number of complaints against developed nations by developing nations **11** increased on year to year (Y-O-Y) basis, so would the number, by them, against their counterparts, increase. basis; however, the number would decrease against their counterparts.

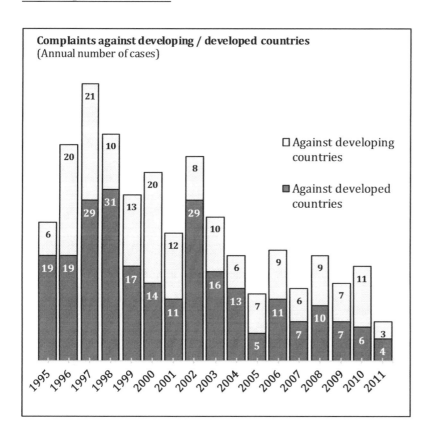

Complaints against developing / developed countries
(Annual number of cases)

☐ Against developing countries

■ Against developed countries

5.2   Passage 2: Gas attacks during WW II

Passage 2

Gas attacks during WW II

Questions 1-11 are based on the following passage.

The attack on Pearl Harbor by the Japanese introduced America to the world theater of World War II. What was unique about this battle was that American citizens **1** expe-rienced it to be   the first attack on American soil in what was then recent memory. Throughout World War I, Americans mostly felt **2** having secured in their homes.   **3** Moreover, the changing times and the audacity of nationalistic world powers, raised questions as to the need for civilian defense.

Germany unleashed the lengthiest bombing campaign of the war on the people of London primarily to weaken British morale. Later, the Allied Forces would fire-bomb the German city of **4** Dresden, housing an almost entirely civilian population and had incidental wartime production.

1. **(A)** NO CHANGE
   (B) experienced it as
   (C) experienced to be
   (D) experienced

2. **(A)** NO CHANGE
   (B) secure
   (C) being secured
   (D) having been secured

3. **(A)** NO CHANGE
   (B) However,
   (C) Consequently,
   (D) Surprisingly,

4. **(A)** NO CHANGE
   (B) Dresden; it had been housed with
   (C) Dresden, having houses for
   (D) Dresden, which had housed

Statistics show that top four country groups— **5** Germany, Russia, USA, and Austria-Hungary—accounted for more than 75% of all battlefield deaths.

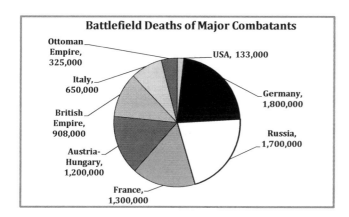

Battlefield Deaths of Major Combatants

Ottoman Empire, 325,000
Italy, 650,000
British Empire, 908,000
Austria-Hungary, 1,200,000
France, 1,300,000
USA, 133,000
Germany, 1,800,000
Russia, 1,700,000

[1] Early, on Britain and the United States enacted an emergency measure to protect their youth population. [2] **6** The highest priority was the protection of children from possible attack. [3] A **7** bulky concern was the exposure to gas attack, an effective measure against unwitting urban dwellers. [4] Immediately after Pearl Harbor, thousands of military training masks were rushed to people living on the islands. **8**

[5] Instead, Hawaiian officials produced an expedient made up of bunny ears and a hood mask. [6] This would lead to further improvisation in the protection of the child civilian population. [7] The Sun Rubber Com-

5. **(A)** NO CHANGE
   (B) Germany, Russia, Italy, and Austria-Hungary
   (C) Germany, Russia, France, and Austria-Hungary
   (D) Germany, Russia, British Empire, and Austria-Hungary

6. For the sake of cohesion of this paragraph, sentence 2, "The highest ... attack" should be
   (A) where it is now
   (B) placed before sentence 1
   (C) placed after sentence 5
   (D) placed before sentence 7

7. **(A)** NO CHANGE
   (B) specific
   (C) tertiary
   (D) looming

8. The writer is considering adding the following sentence here. Should the writer do this?

   > However, the available equipment was unsuitable for protecting children.

   (A) Yes, because 'equipment' mentioned in the sentence refers to children friendly bunny ears and a hood mask.
   (B) Yes, because the sentence sets the purpose of designing children friendly masks.
   (C) No, because it is redundant and interrupts the flow of the paragraph; the unsuitability of masks is discussed later in the paragraph.
   (D) No, because it weakens the focus of the passage by discussing a subject other than masks.

pany designed a mask based on the universal Walt Disney cartoon figure Mickey Mouse; the Mickey Mouse gas mask was then approved by the Chemical Warfare Service of the U.S. Department of Defense, with the assumption that other winning designs could follow the success of this first run. [8] The popularity of Walt Disney cartoon figure Mickey Mouse masks **9** <u>was</u> dependent on internalizing **10** <u>its</u> use in children by making their presence part of a perceived game. [9] **11** <u>This camouflage potentially reduced the element of fear that the masks conveyed to their recipients.</u> If the element of fear could be diminished, gas masks might be employed by their owners more quickly in the event of an attack, and also worn without interruption.

9. **(A)** NO CHANGE
   (B) were
   (C) had been
   (D) which were

10. **(A)** NO CHANGE
    (B) there
    (C) their
    (D) DELETE the word

11. **(A)** NO CHANGE
    (B) This potentially reduced the element of fear that masks' recipients conveyed.
    (C) The reduction of potential element of fear posed upon their recipients was done by masks.
    (D) This camouflage potentially reduced the fear elements of the recipients when they used these masks.

5.3 Passage 3: Sustainability of Homo Sapience

Passage 3

Sustainability of Homo Sapience

Questions 1-11 are based on the following passage.

The positioning of human beings as one of the species with the largest biomasses on earth, **1** and also as the leading influence on earth's ecosystems is the result of the ecological processes which brought **2** upon their migration from the African Savannah, and geographically dispersed them throughout the world. It can be said that rudimentary measure of the success of the species is its position near the top of the aggregate biomass scale. Biomass is the total mass of all **3** lively members of a species. **4** For human beings, it is a reflection of their claim on territory, and their consumption of resources as a species. It might be short-sighted to belittle the success of an emerging species or breed for being small in number if it is evident that the members of the species are elegant and well-adjusted.

5 Unfortunately, the ability to adapt one's habitat to the largest ecosystem, while still retaining the flexibility to deal with local demands on the population may be considered

1. **(A)** NO CHANGE
   (B) also as the leading influence
   (C) and as the leading influence
   (D) and leading the influence

2. **(A)** NO CHANGE
   (B) into
   (C) forth
   (D) about

3. **(A)** NO CHANGE
   (B) live
   (C) alive
   (D) living

4. **(A)** NO CHANGE.
   (B) For human beings there is a reflection of their claim on territory, and the consumption of resources by them as a species.
   (C) For human beings it is a reflection of its claim on territory, and the consumption of resources by it as a species.
   (D) For human beings there are reflections on their claim on territory, and the consumption of resources by them as a species.

5. **(A)** NO CHANGE
   (B) However
   (C) Consequently
   (D) Moreover

high art in the annals of successful adaptation.

It is here that human beings have had nearly unparalleled success (insects being larger in worldwide biomass). As a result, human beings exist in huge numbers. It is the fact that human beings have remained in **6** a generally undifferentiated form that allows them to rank high as a single successful species.

The whole world has been **7** tenanted with life. **8** Human beings are considered unique as they retain their forms as they travel from environment to environment. Historically, human beings, like all organisms, may be driven into new areas, or a new environment may spring up around them as a result of drought, competition or geological changes.

9 Still, human beings have been able to adjust their behavior sufficiently to avoid having nature make such extensive piecemeal adjustments to them that entirely distinct workable alternatives of the same model occupy the new space. **10**

According to the graph given, **11** biomass of only humans and that of wild animals increased.

6. **(A)** NO CHANGE
   (B) a generally differentiated form that allows them to rank high as a single successful species
   (C) a generally undifferentiated form that allows them to rank low as a single successful species
   (D) a generally differentiated form that allows them to rank low as a single successful species

7. Which of the following can BEST describe the underlined word without compromising the meaning?
   (A) hired
   (B) occupied
   (C) rented
   (D) stuffed

8. **(A)** NO CHANGE
   (B) Human beings are unique as they retain their forms while traversing different environments.
   (C) Human beings are considered unique as they retain their forms as they travel all environments.
   (D) Human beings are uniform as they travel across environments.

9. **(A)** NO CHANGE
   (B) Instead
   (C) Comparatively
   (D) Since

10. Which of the following can BEST describe the underlined word without compromising the meaning?
    (A) Yes, because it shows how nature has changed species into a wholly different specimen.
    (B) Yes, because this illustrates how human beings are different from other species and avoided being changed by nature.

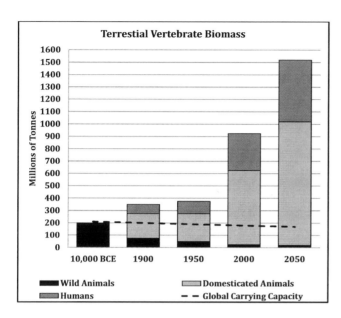

Terrestial Vertebrate Biomass

Legend:
- Wild Animals
- Humans
- Domesticated Animals
- Global Carrying Capacity

(C) No, because it only serves to confuse the reader as to what the author meant by piecemeal adjustments done by nature.

(D) No, because it fails to explain how the mentioned species evolved into others and the reasons for it.

11. **(A)** NO CHANGE

(B) biomass of domesticated animals increased but that of humans and that of wild animals decreased

(C) biomass of wild animals and that of domesticated animals increased but that of humans decreased

(D) biomass of humans and that of domesticated animals increased but that of wild animals decreased

5.4   Passage 4: Lord Dalhousie's reforms in india

Passage 4

Lord Dalhousie's reforms in india

Questions 1-11 are based on the following passage.

The reforms introduced by Lord Dalhousie in India **1** endangering his eight-year stint as the Governor General are many. Dalhousie introduced a new system of internal communication in India. Dalhousie convinced the authorities of the need of the railways and **2** laid down the main lines of their development. He envisaged a network of railways connecting the main places with the ports and **3** providing both for strategic needs and commercial development. Gradually all important cities and towns were linked up with railway lines. The railway lines were not built by the Indian Exchequer but by private English Companies under a system of "Government Guarantee". **4** Besides facilitating trade & commerce and minimizing distances, the railways have gone a long way in uniting India.

1. **(A)** NO CHANGE
   (B) prohibiting
   (C) regarding
   (D) during

2. **(A)** NO CHANGE
   (B) will lay down
   (C) lays down
   (D) is laying down

3. **(A)** NO CHANGE
   (B) for both providing
   (C) providing for together
   (D) providing for both

4. The writer is considering deleting the underlined sentence. Should the writer do this?

   (A) Yes, because it focuses on railways' tertiary objective of unification of India, thus loses the focus on primary objectives of facilitating trade & commerce and minimizing distances in India.

   (B) Yes, because it digresses from the primary focus of the passage, which is the reforms introduced by Dalhousie, and talks of the benefits of railways in the present times.

   (C) No, because it articulates "unification of India" as railways' one of the three objectives.

   (D) No, because it presents "unification of India" as railways' most important objective.

5 [1] Nevertheless, in 1852 Dalhousie introduced the Electric Telegraph System in India. [2] The first telegraph line was from Calcutta to Agra **6** which were opened in 1854, and covered a distance of 800 miles. [3] By 1857, it was extended to Lahore and to Peshawar. [4] Before Lord Dalhousie, military boards were in charge of the construction of Public Works. **7** Hence working civilians were completely neglected by the military board. [5] A separate Public Works Department was established by Lord Dalhousie. [6] Irrigational works were undertaken on an **8** expensive scale. [7] The construction of Ganges Canal was completed and was inaugurated on April 8, 1854. [8] Many bridges and canals were constructed and and the construction of Grand Trunk Road was also taken up.

[9] Dalhousie's special contribution was the construction of an engineering college at Roorkee and in other presidencies. **9**

Most importantly, Lord Dalhousie is credited with the creation of the modern postal system in India. Dalhousie, who held many roles in the administration and internal development of the region, contributed to the Indian postal system doing away with **10** these past

5. (A) NO CHANGE
   (B) Additionally
   (C) However
   (D) As a result

6. (A) NO CHANGE
   (B) which have
   (C) which was
   (D) have

7. (A) NO CHANGE
   (B) Hence Civilian Works were completely neglected by the military board.
   (C) Hence civilians completely neglected the military board.
   (D) Hence works of civilians were completely neglected by the military board.

8. (A) NO CHANGE
   (B) erratic
   (C) universal
   (D) extensive

9. The writer wants to add the following sentences to the paragraph.

   > In Burma, a line was laid down from Rangoon to Mandalay. People could send a message from one place to another place very easily by this telegraph system.

   The best placement for these sentences is immediately

   (A) before sentence 4
   (B) after sentence 5
   (C) after sentence 4
   (D) before sentence 7

10. (A) NO CHANGE

obstructions and levying a uniform rate of postage.

All letters weighing less than a prescribed amount in weight would require the same postal fee (half an Anna) regardless of their destination or origin. This idea of instituting a uniform unit of **11** weighing and of charge for the whole of the vast Indian empire seemed sheer folly to many orthodox financiers of his time. It was, they said, pushing Rowland Hill's scheme of a-penny postage for England to an extreme. For these onlookers, Dalhousie's plan was not so much an extension of the English penny postage scheme, as a reductio ad absurdum of the reform that had been effected in Great Britain. What could be more extravagant or more unjust than to levy the same charge on two letters, one of which was to be delivered to the adjoining street, and the other to the opposite side of India?

    (B) its past
    (C) their past
    (D) DELETE the word

11. **(A)** NO CHANGE
    (B) weighs
    (C) weigh
    (D) weight

5.5   Passage 5: Belgian economy

Passage 5

Belgian economy

Questions 1-11 are based on the following passage.

For 200 years until World War I, French-speaking Wallonia was a technically advanced, indus-trial **1** region. Consequently, Dutch-speaking Flanders was predominantly agricultural. This disparity began to fade during the interwar period. When Belgium emerged from World War II with its industrial infrastructure rela-tively undamaged, mainly because of the Ga-lopin Doctrine, the stage was set for a period of rapid development, particularly in Flan-ders. The older, traditional industries of Wal-lonia, **2** mostly steelmaking, began to lose their competitive edge during this period, but the general growth of world prosperity masked this deterioration until the 1973 and 1979 oil price shocks and resultant shifts in interna-tional demand **3** sent the economy into a period of prolonged recession.

1. **(A)** NO CHANGE
   (B) region, while
   (C) region, on the other hand
   (D) region, and at the same time,

2. **(A)** NO CHANGE
   (B) totally
   (C) particularly
   (D) completely

3. **(A)** NO CHANGE
   (B) for prolonged periods resulted in the economy to sink in deep reces-sion
   (C) lead to a prolonged period of re-cession for the economy
   (D) that led to a prolonged period of recession for the economy

[1] In the 1980s and 1990s, the economic center of the country continued to **4** <u>shift northwards</u> to Flanders. [2] The early 1980s saw the country facing a difficult period of structural adjustment caused by declining demand for its traditional products, deteriorating economic performance, and neglected structural reform. [3] Against this grim backdrop, in 1982, Prime Minister Martens' center-right coalition government formulated an economic recovery program to promote export-led growth by enhancing the competitiveness of Belgium's export industries through an 8.5% devaluation. **5** [4] Consequently, the 1980-82 recession shook Belgium to its core — unemployment rose, social welfare costs increased, **6** <u>personal debt was soaring</u>, the government deficit climbed to 13% of GDP, and the national debt, although mostly held domestically, **7** <u>shrank</u>. [5] Economic growth rose from 2% in 1984 to a peak of 4% in 1989. [6] In May 1990, the government linked the franc to the German Mark, primarily through **8** <u>closely tracking</u> German interest rates. **9**

4. **(A)** NO CHANGE
   (B) rise
   (C) relocate upwards
   (D) increase northwards

5. For the sake of cohesion of this passage, sentence 4 should be
   (A) where it is now
   (B) placed before sentence 2
   (C) placed before sentence 3
   (D) placed after sentence 5.

6. **(A)** NO CHANGE
   (B) personal debt had soared
   (C) personal debt soared
   (D) personal debt had been soaring

7. **(A)** NO CHANGE
   (B) dilated
   (C) dwindle
   (D) mushroomed

8. **(A)** NO CHANGE
   (B) close tracking
   (C) close track
   (D) tracking close

9. The writer wants to add the following sentence to the paragraph.

   > Consequently, as German interest rates rose after 1990, Belgian rates increased and contributed to a decline in the economic growth rate.

   The best placement for the sentence is immediately
   (A) before sentence 6
   (B) after sentence 6
   (C) before sentence 5
   (D) after sentence 3

Although Belgium is a wealthy country, it over-spent income and under-collected taxes for years. The Belgian government reacted to the 1973 and 1979 oil price hikes with poor macroeconomic policies: it transferred workers made redundant in the private sector to the public sector and subsidized ailing **10** industries; coal, steel, textiles, glass, and shipbuilding; in order to prop up the economy.

As a result, cumulative government debt reached 121% of GNP by the end of the 1980s (versus a cumulative U.S. federal public debt/GNP ratio of 31.2% in 1990). **11** However, thanks to Belgium's high personal savings rate, the Belgian Government managed to finance the deficit mainly from domestic savings. This minimized the deleterious effects on the overall economy.

10. **(A)** NO CHANGE

    (B) industries—coal, steel, textiles, glass, and shipbuilding—

    (C) industries: coal, steel, textiles, glass, and shipbuilding;

    (D) industries. Coal, steel, textiles, glass, and shipbuilding;

11. The writer is considering deleting the underlined sentence. Should the writer do this?

    (A) Yes, as it contradicts the essence of the passage which suggests that Belgium was in deep recession

    (B) Yes, as it limits the discussion to Belgium's high personal savings rate while the passage discusses Belgium's economy as a whole

    (C) No, as it elucidates how some "deleterious effects on the overall economy" were minimized

    (D) No, as it substantiates the fact that Belgium was a wealthy country

5.6   Passage 6: Accumulation of Oxygen

Passage 6

Accumulation of Oxygen

Questions 1-11 are based on the following passage.

[1] The earliest accumulation of oxygen in the atmosphere **1** was arguably the most important biological event in Earth history. [2] A general consensus **2** asserts that appreciable oxygen first accumulated in Earth's atmosphere around 2.3 billion years ago during the so-called Great Oxidation Event (GOE). [3] Scientists have long speculated **3** so as to why animal species didn't burgeon sooner even though plants **4** have long started appearing and developing, once sufficient oxygen covered the Earth's surface. [4] Animals first appeared and began to prosper at the end of the Proterozoic period, about 500 to 600 million years ago—but the billion-year stretch before that, when there was also plenty of oxygen, there were no animals. **5**

1. **(A)** NO CHANGE
    (B) is arguably
    (C) being arguably
    (D) had been arguably

2. **(A)** NO CHANGE
    (B) assert
    (C) would assert
    (D) has asserted

3. **(A)** NO CHANGE
    (B) as to
    (C) as though
    (D) DELETE

4. **(A)** NO CHANGE
    (B) long starting to
    (C) long started
    (D) had long started

5. For the sake of cohesion of the first paragraph, sentence 2 should be
    (A) where it is now
    (B) placed before sentence 1
    (C) placed after sentence 3
    (D) placed after sentence 4

Evidently, the air was not oxygen-rich enough then. The oxygen levels during the billion or more years before **6** raising animals were only 0.1 percent of what **7** they are today. In other words, Earth's atmosphere couldn't have supported a diversity of creatures, no matter what genetic advancements were in place. **8** Since there is no question that genetic and ecological innovations are ultimately behind the rise of animals, there is also no question that for animal life to flourish, a certain level of oxygen is required. **9**

The evidence was found by analyzing chromium isotopes in ancient sediments from China, Australia, Canada, and the United States. Chromium is found in the Earth's continental crust, and chromium oxidation, the process recorded by the chromium isotopes, **10** are directly linked to the presence of free oxygen in the atmosphere.

Specifically, samples **11** were deposited near the ancient shoreline in shallow, iron-rich ocean areas were studied and compared with other samples taken from younger shoreline locales deposited in similar settings but known to have higher levels of oxygen.

6. (A) NO CHANGE
   (B) the rise of
   (C) rising
   (D) the raise of

7. (A) NO CHANGE
   (B) it is
   (C) the levels are
   (D) there are

8. (A) NO CHANGE
   (B) While
   (C) If
   (D) Despite

9. The writer is considering deleting the underlined sentence. Should the sentence be kept or deleted?

   (A) Keep, because it provides a detail that supports the main topic of the paragraph.
   (B) Keep, because it presents a fact based on which the rest of the paragraph follows.
   (C) Delete, because it blurs the paragraph's main focus with loosely related details.
   (D) Delete, because it provides a detail that has been provided in the earlier paragraph.

10. (A) NO CHANGE
    (B) directly linked
    (C) has been directly linked
    (D) is directly linked

11. (A) NO CHANGE
    (B) had been
    (C) had
    (D) DELETE

5.7   Passage 7: Fast food and obesity

Passage 7

Fast food and obesity

Questions 1-11 are based on the following passage.

[1] Studies show that **1** obesity is increasing rapidly across all age groups. [2] Recent evidence from scientists has shown that eating "fast food" can be addictive in much the same way as using controlled substances can be. [3] The proposed conclusions contend that the brains of **2** overeaters experienced chemical changes in response to unbalanced diets with a high content of processed sugar, salt, and saturated fats. [4] According to researchers, "fast food", such as hamburgers, processed sugar, and a wide range of deep fried foods, can trigger a dependency in the brain that perpetuates a habit of further use. [5] It is a view that is increasingly supported by scientists who see a co-dependency between people's decisions and environmental influences (including the wide availability of people's favorite "fast foods") **3** that have structural effects on human development. **4**

In time and in some cases, if people continue a pattern of consumption containing

1. Which of the following CANNOT replace the underlined phrase to convey the desired meaning?

   (A) obesity is increasing at a rapid pace across
   (B) obesity is increasing very rapidly across
   (C) obesity is rapidly increasing across
   (D) obesity is rising at a rapid rate throughout

2. (A) NO CHANGE
   (B) overeaters experience chemical changes
   (C) overeaters had experienced chemical changes
   (D) overeaters experience chemically changed

3. (A) NO CHANGE
   (B) who have structural effects
   (C) which have structural affects
   (D) that has structural effect

4. For the sake of cohesion of this paragraph, sentence 3 should be
   (A) where it is now
   (B) placed before sentence 1
   (C) placed after sentence 1
   (D) placed after sentence 5

too much unhealthy food, **5** their intake of this food will initiate changes in **6** the brain that elevates the minimum level of ingestion the brain needs for satiation. Moreover, since high consumption of "fast foods" stimulates opiates in the brain (substances which act as natural pain relievers), large, recurrent doses of "fast food" can **7** mimic the effects of opiates, albeit in a less intense form. **8** Scientists raising rats on a diet of twenty-five percent sugar found that upon suddenly eliminating glucose from the rats' food supply, the animals experienced all the symptoms of withdrawal attributed to reducing traditional addictive opiates, including shivering and chattering teeth.

5. **(A)** NO CHANGE

   (B) their intakes of these foods

   (C) its intake of this food

   (D) their intakes of this food

6. **(A)** NO CHANGE

   (B) the brain, elevating

   (C) the brain having elevated

   (D) the elevated brain

7. Which of the following can replace the underlined phrase to convey nearly the same meaning effectively?

   (A) replace the ill-effects

   (B) play the role

   (C) alleviate the effect

   (D) eliminate the effects

8. The writer is considering deleting the underlined sentence. Should the sentence be kept or deleted?

   (a) Yes, because the paragraph talks about the effects of opiates in human brain, thus discussing the effects of opiates in the context of rat loses the focus.

   (b) Yes, because the passage discusses effects of high consumption of fast foods, such as processed sugar, salt, and saturated fats, whereas the sentence is skewed to the effects of no consumption of sugar.

   (c) No, because by citing the experiment on rats, scientist wished to drive a point that if the symptoms can occur with rats, so they can with humans.

   (d) No, because mimicking the effects of opiates experiment carried with rats is not possible with humans.

Later, by treating rats with drugs that block opiate receptors, scientists were able to lower the amount of dopamine in the nucleus acumen of rats' brains, an area linked with the dynamics of reward. Such neurochemistry can be seen in heroin addicts coping with withdrawal. By this reasoning, obesity, **9** like other addictions, can be viewed as a disease beyond the control of those afflicted by it.

[1] This has brought lawyers to argue that civil society has a responsibility to regulate food **10** and educating people about the abuse of "unhealthy foods" in a way that is comparable to society's control of opiates and narcotics. [2] Corporations that target this vulnerability in human beings can then be held liable for the sicknesses that result from the poor eating habits overwhelming their customers. [3] For these researchers, the distinction between a habit and an addiction is not quantitative but qualitative. [4] Their consensus is that individuals can still moderate their behavior to control the effects of what they eat on their systems. **11**

9. (A) NO CHANGE
   (B) unlike
   (C) as
   (D) such as

10. (A) NO CHANGE
    (B) thereby educating people
    (C) and educate people
    (D) and hence educate people

11. The writer wants to add the following sentence to the third paragraph.

    > Still, some scientists scoff at the lengths to which their colleagues seek to separate the decision making process from people's behavior.

    The best placement for the sentence is immediately

    (A) before sentence 1
    (B) after sentence 1
    (C) before sentence 3
    (D) after sentence 3

5.8 Passage 8: In-fighting princes

Passage 8

In-fighting princes

Questions 1-11 are based on the following passage.

[1] For 17th century Europeans, the history of Eastern monarchies, **1** such as everything else in Asia, was stereotyped and invariable. [2] According to similar typical accounts of Indian events, history **2** displayed itself as the predictable rituals of heavy-handed folklore. [3] Typically, the founder of a dynasty, a brave soldier, is a desperate intriguer, and **3** expels from the throne the feeble and degenerate scions of a more ancient house. [4] This founder's son may inherit some of the talent of the father; but in two or three generations luxury and indolence **4** does its work, and the feeble inheritors of a great name are dethroned by some new adventurer, destined to bequeath a like misfortune to his degenerate **5** descendants. [5] Thus rebellion and deposition were the correctives of despotism, and therefore, a recurrence, at fixed intervals, of able and vigorous princes through the medium of periodical anarchy and civil war, **6** was occurring . [6] It was this perception of history that allowed Britain's

1. **(A)** NO CHANGE
   (B) like
   (C) similar as
   (D) same as

2. **(A)** NO CHANGE
   (B) repeated itself
   (C) unfolded itself with
   (D) folded within itself

3. **(A)** NO CHANGE
   (B) evacuates the throne of
   (C) dethrones from the throne
   (D) uproots from the throne

4. **(A)** NO CHANGE
   (B) does their
   (C) do its
   (D) do their

5. **(A)** NO CHANGE
   (B) descendants. Thus,
   (C) descendants, thus,
   (D) descendants; thus,

6. **(A)** NO CHANGE

rulers **7** <u>to lie</u> claim to the governance of the subcontinent. [7] This claim justified British policy, as well as dictated how they thought about gaining the favor of India's local monarchies. [8] The rationale that justified their actions to the British public was that avoiding such upheaval to allow peaceful reign over India was their ultimate goal. [9] <u>The British claimed to be interested in avoiding these periods of bloodshed.</u> **8**

[1] British armies and British administrators **9** <u>were able to insinuate</u> rule over India by two primary methods. [2] The first of these was the outright annexation of Indian states and subsequent direct governance of the underlying regions subsequently. [3] The second form of asserting power involved treaties in which Indian rulers acknowledged the Company's hegemony in return for limited internal autonomy. [4] The most important such support came from the subsidiary alliances with Indian princes during the first 75 years of Company rule. [5] The British achieved this by setting up native princes in positions of power. [6] Their methods took advantage of existing "doctrines of lapse", and made use of what was already the declared law in cases of heredity. [7] By the Doctrine of Lapse,

(B) had been occurring

(C) had occurred

(D) occurred

7. **(A)** NO CHANGE

   (B) to lay

   (C) laying

   (D) to have laid

8. For the sake of cohesion of this paragraph, sentence 9 should be

   (A) where it is now

   (B) placed after sentence 7

   (C) placed before sentence 7

   (D) placed before sentence 6

9. Which of the following can replace the underlined phrase to convey nearly the same meaning effectively?

   (A) NO CHANGE

   (B) tried to enter into

   (C) were able to enjoy

   (D) monopolized their

if the king of a subordinate state died without a natural male heir, then the kingdom would 'lapse' to the British i.e. it would automatically pass into the hands of the British. [8] By intervening on behalf of one prince or another, both of whom may have been equally suited to claim the right to the throne in cases in which the rights to leadership lapsed, they put themselves in a position to support a leader they selected, and to maintain his power as long as it was in their interests. **11**

10. **(A)** NO CHANGE

    (B) British, i.e.

    (C) British, ie,

    (D) British, i.e.,

11. The writer wants to add the following sentence to this paragraph.

    > Since the Company operated under financial constraints, it had to set up political underpinnings for its rule.

    The best placement for the sentence is immediately

    (a) before sentence 6

    (b) after sentence 1

    (c) before sentence 3

    (d) before sentence 4

5.9   Passage 9: Abortion Law

Passage 9
Abortion Law

Questions 1-11 are based on the following passage.

The question of legalized abortion in America has largely been considered in terms of moral objections resulting from **1** compelling perceptions of human rights and freedom of choice. While the representatives of these views have been influential actors for whom lawmakers must tweak any legislation **2** pertains with abortion, economists now offer tangible evidence that the abortion issue must be evaluated with some very practical considerations as well. **3** Inasmuch as the importance of the life of a foetus brought-to-term is never a forgotten aspect of the debate on abortion, the relevance of the abortion issue to the lifestyle opportunities for all of society has yet to be weighed heavily in the debate.

However, in their retrospective examination of many years' evidence, John Donahue and Steven Levitt, researchers from Harvard University and the University of Chicago, **4** pointing out that a suggested correlation

1. **(A)** NO CHANGE

   (B) competitive perceptions

   (C) complementary perceptions

   (D) competing perceptions

2. **(A)** NO CHANGE

   (B) pertains with

   (C) pertaining to

   (D) pertaining with

3. **(A)** NO CHANGE

   (B) While

   (C) Since

   (D) However,

between the passage of Roe vs. Wade, the integral piece of abortion empowerment legislation, and reported crime statistics twenty years later can in fact be noted. This is because the period during which most perpetrators engage in the majority of any society's illegal activity is when they are in their late teens and early twenties. Adolescent and young adult males are considered to be the most likely to engage in illegal activities. Their relative inexperience in the world, the paucity of opportunities and their group relationships make them more prone to violence and defiance than women or older males. The researchers note that within a few years of the U.S. Supreme Court Roe vs. Wade decision, up to a quarter of all pregnancies in the United States resulted in abortions. Also, they observe that crime rates between 1985 and 1997 declined. The researchers note that children who **5** had otherwise been born in the early years after the Roe vs. Wade decision would be reaching their late teen years between 1985 and 1997. However, they were not born, **6** therefore crime decreased in this time frame. These researchers interpret the termination of an unwanted pregnancy as the rational response of a woman who is not prepared to **7** provide care for a child. Going forward with an unwanted pregnancy

4. (A) NO CHANGE
   (B) are pointing
   (C) had pointed
   (D) have pointed

5. (A) NO CHANGE
   (B) would have otherwise been
   (C) have otherwise been
   (D) were otherwise

6. (A) NO CHANGE
   (B) thus
   (C) hence
   (D) so

presumably confers on the woman too great a challenge in raising a child she is poorly prepared **8** for, providing the child with an upbringing **9** where is suboptimal, making him more vulnerable to be party to illegal conduct.

[1] These numbers signify less crime as a result of letting more mothers choose when to have a baby. [2] Crime is financially costly to taxpayers as well. [3] As the ideological **10** arguments of abortion refuse to abate, it may be time for hamstrung legislators to consider new sources of information to simplify their decisions about reopening the question of abortion reform and government aid. **11**

7. **(A)** NO CHANGE
   (B) care for
   (C) care about
   (D) care less for

8. **(A)** NO CHANGE
   (B) for; and provides
   (C) for, and provides
   (D) for, and providing

9. **(A)** NO CHANGE
   (B) when
   (C) which
   (D) that

10. **(A)** arguments of
    (B) arguments against
    (C) arguments over
    (D) arguments for

11. The writer wants to add the following sentence to the paragraph.

    > Lawmakers may take heed of this evaluation if they consider Donahue and Levitt's calculation that the economic benefit to society from the termination of unwanted pregnancies may be as high as $30 billion annually.

    The best placement for the sentence is immediately

    (A) before sentence 1
    (B) after sentence 1
    (C) after sentence 2
    (D) after sentence 3

5.10 Passage 10: Proteins Therapeutics

Passage 10

Proteins Therapeutics

Questions 1-11 are based on the following passage.

Once a rarely used subset of medical treatments, **1** the use of protein therapeutics has increased dramatically in number and frequency of use since the introduction of the first recombinant **2** protein therapeutic–human insulin– 25 years ago. Protein therapeutics already have a significant role in almost every field of medicine **3** but this role is still only in its infancy. Human proteins, **4** such as erythropoietin, granulocyte colony–stimulating factor and alpha-L-iduronidase, are in great demand for the treatment of a variety of diseases. Some can be purified from **5** blood, this is expensive and runs the risk of contamination by AIDS or hepatitis C. **6** Proteins can be produced in human cell culture but costs are very high and output small.

1. (A) No CHANGE
   (B) protein therapeutics have
   (C) protein therapeutics' use has
   (D) the importance of protein therapeutics has

2. (A) NO CHANGE
   (B) protein therapeutic; human insulin
   (C) protein therapeutic, human insulin
   (D) protein therapeutic human insulin

3. (A) NO CHANGE
   (B) , but
   (C) , however,
   (D) yet

4. (A) NO CHANGE
   (B) like
   (C) such as like
   (D) like as

5. (A) NO CHANGE
   (B) blood, moreover, this
   (C) blood; however, this
   (D) blood, inasmuch as this

6. (A) NO CHANGE
   (B) Proteins can be produced in human cell culture but its costs are very high and output is low.
   (C) Proteins can be produced in human cell culture but the production cost is very high and the output small.

7 <u>Much larger quantities</u> can be produced in bacteria or yeast but the proteins produced can be difficult to purify and they lack the appropriate post-translational modifications that are needed for efficacy in vivo. The table shows that there are as many as **8** <u>three therapeutic proteins that can be used to cure cancer; however only two are commercially available</u> .

(D) Proteins can be produced in human cell culture but their costs are very high and output too low.

7. **(A)** NO CHANGE

   (B) Much large quantities

   (C) Many larger quantities

   (D) Too much quantities

Protein	Trade name	Therapeutic function	Development
Rasburicase	Elitek	Hyperuricemia	Commercially available
Reteplase (tissue plasminogen factor)	Retavase	Acute myocardial infarction	Commercially available
Thyroid stimulating hormone	Thyrogen	Thyroid cancer	Commercially available
TNF-alpha	Oncophage	Colorectal, renal cell cancer, melanoma	Phase II
Transtuzumab	Herceptin	HER2 over expressing metastatic breast cancer	Commercially available

8. **(A)** NO CHANGE

   (B) two therapeutic proteins that can be used to cure cancer; however, only two are commercially available.

   (C) three therapeutic proteins that can be used to cure cancer; moreover, all are commercially available.

[1] By contrast, **9** <u>human proteins have appropriate post-translational modifications</u> can be produced in the milk of transgenic sheep, goats, cattle, pigs, rabbits and chickens. [2] The animals are used as sterile bioreactors to produce large, complex proteins or proteins that can't be made in other cell systems. [3] Currently, research groups around the world are investigating **10** <u>whether these transgenic animals can be used</u> to produce therapeutic proteins. [4] Output can be as high as 40 g per liter of milk and costs are relatively low. **11**

(D) at least three therapeutic proteins that can be used to cure cancer; however, only one is commercially available.

9. **(A)** NO CHANGE

   (B) human proteins that have appropriate post-translational modifications

   (C) human proteins which have appropriate post-translational modifications

   (D) human proteins, having appropriate post-translational modifications

10. **(A)** NO CHANGE

    (B) whether those transgenic animals can be used

    (C) whether these animals that have transgenic characteristics can be used

    (D) whether these animals that are transgenic can be used

11. For the sake of cohesion of this paragraph, sentence 3 should be

    (A) where it is now

    (B) placed before sentence 1

    (C) placed after sentence 1

    (D) placed after sentence 4

Chapter 6

Answer Key

Passage 1: Role of WTO

(1) A	(3) B	(5) C	(7) B	(9) D	(11) C
(2) B	(4) B	(6) B	(8) A	(10) A	

Passage 2: Gas attacks during WW II

(1) B	(3) B	(5) C	(7) D	(9) A	(11) A
(2) B	(4) D	(6) A	(8) B	(10) C	

Passage 3: Sustainability of Homo Sapience

(1) C	(3) D	(5) B	(7) B	(9) A	(11) D
(2) D	(4) A	(6) A	(8) B	(10) B	

Passage 4: Lord Dalhousie's reforms in india

(1) D	(3) D	(5) B	(7) B	(9) A	(11) D
(2) A	(4) C	(6) C	(8) D	(10) B	

Passage 5: Belgian economy

(1) B	(3) A	(5) C	(7) D	(9) B	(11) C
(2) C	(4) A	(6) C	(8) A	(10) B	

Passage 6: Accumulation of Oxygen

(1) B	(3) B	(5) A	(7) C	(9) B	(11) D
(2) A	(4) D	(6) B	(8) B	(10) D	

Passage 7: Fast food and obesity

(1) B	(3) A	(5) A	(7) B	(9) A	(11) C
(2) B	(4) D	(6) B	(8) C	(10) C	

Passage 8: In-fighting princes

(1) B	(3) A	(5) B	(7) B	(9) A	(11) D
(2) C	(4) D	(6) D	(8) C	(10) D	

Passage 9: Abortion Law

(1) D	(3) B	(5) B	(7) B	(9) D	(11) C
(2) C	(4) D	(6) D	(8) C	(10) C	

Passage 10: Proteins Therapeutics

(1) B	(3) B	(5) C	(7) A	(9) B	(11) C
(2) A	(4) A	(6) D	(8) A	(10) A	

Chapter 7

Solutions - Practice Questions

7.1   Passage 1: Role of WTO

Passage 1

Role of WTO

1. This is a question on Idiomatic usage.

   Let us bring out the sentence, "*Experience demonstrates that environmental standards and cleaner production are compatible <u>with</u> and supportive of economic growth.*"

   Option A is the correct answer because 'compatible with' is the correct idiom, and not "of" or "to." Also, using "with" with "compatible" is necessary. The other options are incorrect.

   The correct answer is A.

2. This is a question on usage of pronouns.

   Let us bring out the sentence, "*This link between economic growth and environmental improvement is enshrined, together with the commitment to development, in the World Trade Organization's Preamble, <u>that</u> includes sustainable development as a basic objective of the trading system.*"

   Option B is the correct answer because since the underlined portion is preceded by a comma, 'that' cannot be preceded by a comma whereas 'which' can.

   "Which" and "that"

	Which	**That**
Structure	Noun, which ...	Noun that... [no punctuation between "noun" and "that"
Nature	Universal	Subset, restrictive
	Dogs, which ... [whatever you say has to be true for ALL dogs]	Dogs that ... [whatever you say has to be true only for SOME dogs, NOT ALL dogs]
	Dogs, which are animals, are nice [all dogs are animals and all dogs are nice]	Dogs that are brown are nice [not all dogs are brown, some dogs are brown and such dogs are nice]

   In the given sentence, "WTO's Preamble" has to be followed by "which" because we are referring to the one WTO's Preamble (only one is present in the world – universal). Ask yourself – is there a WTO's Preamble that does not include sustainable development as a basic objective? No, because all WTO's Preambles (since there is only one) do include sustainable development as a basic objective. Thus, "which" is appropriate but not "that."

   Option C is incorrect because 'where' is suitable to refer to a place, whereas 'Preamble' is not a place but is a document or an object.

   Option D is incorrect because 'who' can refer a person, and not to a 'Preamble'.

   The correct answer is B.

3. This is a question on grammatical and clear construction.

   Let us bring out the sentence, "*In endorsing this concept, despite some reservations, WTO members unanimously recognized that trade and the <u>economic growth the WTO helps to create must be fostered</u> in the context of sustainable development which integrates economic, social and environmental policies.*"

   Options A and C are incorrect because the adjectival clause "the WTO helps to create" needs a relative pronoun "that" to link it to the noun "trade and economic growth."

   Also, option C contains the incorrect idiom "create in."

   Option D is incorrect because the adjectival clause "the WTO helps in creation of" is awkward compared to the adjectival clause "the WTO helps to create."

   The correct answer is B.

4. This is a question on expression of ideas.

   Let us bring out the related sentences, "*In endorsing this concept, despite some reservations, WTO members unanimously recognized that trade and the economic growth that WTO helps to create must be fostered* in the context of sustainable development which integrates economic, social and environmental policies. 4 Economic growth, sustainable development, and opportunity for citizens are fundamental goals of every society."

   Option C is the correct answer because the passage is about the role of WTO and an irrelevant and unnecessary reference to the IMF is uncalled for.

   The correct answer is C.

5. This is a question on transition words.

   Let us bring out the related sentences, "*Economic growth, sustainable development, and opportunity for citizens are fundamental goals of every society. <u>And the record</u> of the past five decades clearly shows how the trading system has helped us reach some of these goals.*"

   Option C is the correct answer because the sentence, "*...the record of the past five decades clearly shows how the trading system has helped us reach some of these goals.*" does not contrast the previous sentence "Economic growth, sustainable development, and opportunity for citizens are fundamental goals of every society." The second sentence builds upon the point made by the earlier sentence, while the usage of 'However' implies contrast, changing the meaning.

   The correct answer is C.

6. This is a question on subject-verb agreement.

   Let us bring out the sentence, "*Since 1960, the WTO has negotiated a 90% drop in tariffs, and non-tariff barriers to trade <u>has</u> also been dramatically reduced.*"

   What has been dramatically reduced? The non-tariff barriers have been reduced. Thus, the subject of the second clause is the plural "non-tariff barriers."

   Option B is the correct answer because 'have been' agrees with a plural subject 'non-tariff barriers.'

   Option C is incorrect because "would" is used for hypothetical events whereas the given sentence is not hypothetical but is real.

Option D is incorrect because without any conjugate verb, the sentence would be grammatically incorrect. Every clause must contain a properly matched subject and verb.

The correct answer is B.

7. This is a question on idiomatic construction.

Let us bring out the sentence, "*Moreover, market access for agriculture and services will be further expanded <u>upon concluding</u> the next Uruguay Round.*"

The sentence wishes to state that once the Uruguay Round is done, market access will be further expanded. Thus, the correct meaning to convey for the underlined phrase is "after the Uruguay Round is concluded."

Option A is incorrect because using the phrase "concluding" is incorrect since the actual subject of "conclude" is not present in the sentence. Who will conclude the Uruguay round? WTO will conclude. If the sentence were "WTO will expand market access ..." we could have said "WTO will expand market access ... upon/after concluding ..." However, in the absence of the correct subject, such a phrase cannot be used.

Option B is the correct answer because it conveys the correct meaning of the sentence in tone with the existing passive structure of the sentence.

Options C and D are incorrect because by using "for" and "in", they are conveying incorrect meaning: the meaning is "after" not "in" (during) or "for" (because of).

The correct answer is B.

8. This is a question on organization of ideas.

Let us bring out the paragraph, "*[1] Since 1960, the WTO has negotiated a 90% drop in tariffs, and non-tariff barriers to trade have also been dramatically reduced. [2] Moreover, market access for agriculture and services will be further expanded upon conclusion of the next Uruguay Round. [3] Thus, since 1960 trade has grown fifteen-fold; world economic production has quadrupled; and world per capita income has more than doubled. [4] However, has the World Trade Organization done enough to promote sustainable development and protect the environment? The answer is yet to be presented by the WTO.*"

This is a classic paragraph which has four sentences and each starts with a transition or signal word. Sentence 1 starts with 'Since', sentence 2 with 'Moreover', sentence 2 with 'Thus', and sentence 4 with 'However'.

Sentences 1 and 2 articulate what the WTO has done since 1960 for the expansion of trade, market access for agriculture, and services; sentence 3 is a conclusion of the previous sentences; it puts quantitative figures for trade; thus, the placement of sentence 3 is correct. It cannot follow sentence 4 because sentence 4 suggests that the WTO has not done enough to promote sustainable development and protect the environment–a different aspect, altogether.

The correct answer is A.

9. This is a question on sentence construction.

Let us bring out the sentence, "*In reference to the concept of sustainable development, <u>the Brundtland Commission Report of 1987,</u> "we must meet the needs of the present without compromising the ability of future generations to meet their own needs.*"

The first part of the sentence "In reference ... development" is the introductory phrase set off by a comma. The next part has to be the subject and the verb for the sentence in order to make a proper sentence. The subject can be "The Brundtland Commission Report of 1987" and the verb can be "stated" and the part within the inverted commas can be the object of the verb "stated." Only then the sentence is complete and without the subject and the verb, it is a fragment.

Option D is the correct answer because only it provides the subject and the verb needed to make the sentence complete.

The correct answer is D.

10. This is a question on sentence construction.

Let us bring out the sentence, "*Taking into account state practice, treaty law, international case law and relevant legal literature, economists have found that sustainable development is not yet a norm of international law.*"

Option A is the correct answer because a singular verb 'is' agrees with a singular subject 'sustainable development.'

Options B and C are incorrect because they contain the plural verb "are" for the singular subject "sustainable development." Also, putting a conjunction between the subject "sustainable development" and its verb "are" is incorrect in option C.

Option D is incorrect because it is illogical to say that "Taking into account [these four aspects], economists have found that sustainable development is ~~not~~ yet a norm of international law." The original sentence and the context imply that it is **not** yet a norm. Thus, the change is the meaning is not warranted.

The correct answer is A.

11. This is a question on understanding tables and graphs.

Let us bring out the sentence, "*from the beginning, whenever the number of complaints against developed nations by developing nations <u>increased on year to year (Y-O-Y) basis, so would the number, by them, against their counterparts, increase.</u>*"

The sentence means that whenever the number of complaints against developed nations by developing nations increased from any year to the subsequent year, the number of complaints against ~~developed~~ developing nations by ~~developing~~ developed nations in-creased also increased during the same period.

Option C is the correct answer because though above is true *most* of the time, there are a few exceptions, one such: 1997-1998: the number of complaints increased from 29 to 31 against developed nations, but the same for their counterparts decreased from 21 to 10. Another such year is 2001-2002.

The correct answer is C.

7.2   Passage 2: Gas attacks during WW II

Passage 2
Gas attacks during WW II

1. This is a question on the usage of idioms and on sentence structure.

   Let us bring out the sentence, "*What was unique about this battle was that American citizens experienced it to be the first attack on American soil in what was then recent memory.*"

   Option B is the correct answer because 'experienced as' is idiomatically correct and the "it" is necessary to make a proper dependent clause. For example: My experience as (not "to be") a hitchhiker taught me a great deal about human behavior.

   Options C and D are incorrect because after "that" a dependent clause is necessary for the verb "was". Without "it" there will be no object for the verb "experienced", making it incomplete. Thus, an object "it" (referring to "this battle") is necessary.

   Option A and C are incorrect because 'experienced to be' is idiomatically incorrect.

   The correct answer is B.

2. This is a question on the usage of verb and tenses.

   Let us bring out the sentence, "*Throughout World War I, Americans mostly **felt** having secured in their homes.*"

   Whatever verb form we choose has to be in sync with "felt"; Continuous tenses cannot be paired with simple past tense "felt" – "felt having secured", "felt being secured" or "felt having been secured" is incorrect. Options A, C and D contain this error.

   Option B is the correct answer because '*Americans mostly felt secure in their homes*' is grammatically correct and conveys the intended meaning.

   Note: After using a verb in past tense, one cannot pair that past verb with another past tense verb, as in, it is incorrect to say "Americans felt secured" or "I did not went there". After using past tense "felt" or "did", one has to use the bare infinitive form, that is, "Americans felt secure" or "I did not go there."

   Infinitive = to verb; bare infinitive = verb (without "to")

   The correct answer is B.

3. This is a question on the usage of transition words.

   Let us bring out the related sentences, "*Throughout World War I, Americans mostly felt secure in their homes. Moreover, the changing times and the audacity of nationalistic world powers, raised questions as to the need for civilian defense.*"

   'Moreover' is used as a transition word between the two sentences, [1] "*Throughout World War I, Americans mostly felt secure in their homes.*' and [2] '*the changing times and the audacity of nationalistic world powers, raised questions as to the need for civilian defense.*"

   "Moreover" is incorrect because it is used to add *further, supporting* points to the original points and is not meant for contrasting points.

Since sentence 1 discusses lack of the need for civilian defense by suggesting that Americans had felt secure then, it should contrast sentence 2, which implies a need for civilian defense by suggesting that Americans are **not** necessarily **safe** now. Thus, option B, 'However' is an appropriate transition word and is the correct answer.

Usage of 'Consequently' implies that 'changing times' were a result of 'Americans feeling secure in their homes . . . ', which is an illogical inference.

'Surprisingly' is used to add surprising information to what is already said or written, but it is illogical to use here because the second statement is not as much of a surprise as it is a contrast.

The correct answer is B.

4. This is a question on grammatical construction.

   Let us bring out the sentence, "*Later, the Allied Forces would fire-bomb the German city of Dresden, housing an almost entirely civilian population and had incidental wartime production.*"

   What's housing an entirely civilian population? The German city of Dresden is housing an entirely civilian population.

   Thus, to make the clause "house an entirely civilian population" refer to the noun "the German city of Dresden," we have to use a "which" modifier.

   Using an absolute modifier (sentence, verb-ing…) will wrongly indicate that the "housing" part is an effect of the entire sentence before it. However, the "housing" part needs to refer to merely Dresden and not to the entire sentence.

   Examples:

   Correct: The volcano exploded violently, blotting out the sun. [The absolute modifier "blotting out the sun" describes the entire sentence "the volcano exploded violently". Such absolute modifiers can be used to describe an effect of the entire sentence or to provide further details of the actions of the previous sentence.

   Correct: John applied himself to the job completely, arriving early every morning and leaving late every night. [Absolute modifier *providing further details on how* John applied himself to his job]

   Correct: The dolphin family contains the animal known as <u>killer whale, which</u> is an aggressive hunter. [which clause describing the noun before it – killer whale]

   Correct: The dolphin family contains the animal known as killer whale, making it a misnamed family. [the phrase "making it a misnamed family" is referring to the entire clause about "dolphin family containing a whale" and the phrase is not referring to "killer whale"]

   Also, since the clause in the latter part of the sentence '*. . . had incidental wartime production.*' has verb 'had', thus the first part must be parallel to it because of the conjunction "and."

   Though both options B and D have 'had', option D is the correct answer because in option B, '*it (Dresden) had been housed with*' is wrongly written in passive voice, implying that Dresden has been put up with people instead of implying that Dresden itself contains people. Also, using a semicolon instead of continuing the sentence with a modifier incorrectly implies that the thought about Dresden was completed. However, the sentence clearly indicates that the clauses about "housing civilians and having wartime production" are part of important information on Dresden because of which the Allied Forces bombed it.

The correct answer is D.

5. This is a question on the understanding tables and graphs.

By looking at the pie-chart, it looks that it is a calculation-based question and may eat up your precious time; however it is not. This is a logic-based question.

Note that all the options list only four countries. Among all countries, the four countries with the highest number of battlefield deaths, from highest count to lowest count, are Germany, Russia, France, and Austria-Hungary. It is obvious that the percentage of total number of deaths for these four countries compared with that for any other pair of four countries would be higher. Thus if an option lists Germany, Russia, France, and Austria-Hungary, it would be the correct answer.

We see that option C lists Germany, Russia, France, and Austria-Hungary, thus it is the correct answer.

For the sake of your curiosity, let us do the calculation.

The total number of deaths for Germany, Russia, France, and Austria-Hungary equals 6 million and the total of deaths for all the countries equals 8.01 million; so $\frac{6}{8.01} * 100\% = 75\%$.

The correct answer is C.

6. This is a question on organization of ideas.

Let us bring out the related sentences, "*[1] Early on, Britain and the United States enacted an emergency measure to protect their youth population. [2] The highest priority was the protection of children from possible attack. [3] A colossal concern was the exposure to gas attack, an effective measure against unwitting urban dwellers. [4] Immediately after Pearl Harbor, thousands of military training masks were rushed to people living on the islands. [5] Instead, Hawaiian officials produced an expedient made up of bunny ears and a hood mask. [6] This would lead to further improvisation in the protection of the child civilian population. [7] The Sun Rubber Company designed a mask based on the universal Walt Disney cartoon figure Mickey Mouse; the Mickey Mouse gas mask was then approved by the Chemical Warfare Service of the U.S. Department of Defense, with the assumption that other winning designs could follow the success of this first run.*"

The underlined sentence 2 'The highest priority was the protection of children from possible attack' talks about **the protection of children**, and sentence 4 mentions about the dispatch of military training masks, thus it is logical to talk about issue of **the protection of children** before sentence 4. Since there is no option as 'placed before sentence 4', the best placement is 'where it is now'.

Also, sentence 2 cannot be placed before sentence 1 because sentence 1 introduces the point about protection of population, after which one can talk about protecting the children as the highest priority. So, option B is incorrect.

Placing sentence 2 after sentence 5 or sentence 7, would make the term 'highest priority' lose its significance.

The correct answer is A.

7. This is a question on the usage of words and phrases.

   Let us bring out the sentence, "*A bulky concern was the exposure to gas attack, an effective measure against unwitting urban dwellers.*"

   In the sentence '*A bulky concern was the exposure to gas attack, an effective measure against unwitting urban dwellers*', contextually the underlined word should mean primary, important, immediate, serious, weighty, etc. Though 'colossal' mean heavy/weighty, it is an adjective which is used to describe tangible objects, and saying '*colossal concern*' is inappropriate.

   'Looming', meaning approaching/imminent as well as large and distorted, is the correct answer. 'Tertiary', meaning third in order or level implies that the concern is of low importance, which is incorrect. Though 'specific' is not outright incorrect, given a choice between 'specific' and 'looming', 'looming' is a better choice as it maintains the original tone of the sentence with the appropriate word.

   The correct answer is D.

8. This is a question on expression of ideas.

   Let us bring out the related sentences, "[1] *Early on, Britain and the United States enacted an emergency measure to protect their youth population. [2] The highest priority was the protection of children from possible attack. [3] A looming concern was the exposure to gas attack, an effective measure against unwitting urban dwellers. [4] Immediately after Pearl Harbor, thousands of military training masks were rushed to people living on the islands.* **8** [*5] Instead, Hawaiian officials produced an expedient made up of bunny ears and a hood mask. [6] This would lead to further improvisation in the protection of the child civilian population.*"

   Option B is the correct answer because it the sentence '*However, the available equipment was unsuitable for protecting children.*' sets the purpose of designing children friendly masks. After this sentence, author talks about designing children-friendly masks, thus the sentence '*However, the available equipment was unsuitable for protecting children*' logically sets the purpose. Also, the word "instead" in sentence 5 is contrasting very well the idea given in this sentence: this sentence says that even though masks were rushed to people, these were **unsuitable**, and **instead** another type was made for the children.

   Option A presents incorrect information. 'equipment' mentioned in the sentence does not refer to children friendly bunny ears and a hood mask, but to the military mask.

   The correct answer is B.

9. This is a question on verb, agreement and tenses.

   Let us bring out the sentence, "*The popularity of Walt Disney cartoon figure Mickey Mouse masks was dependent on internalizing its use in children by making their presence part of a perceived game.*"

   In the sentence, the underlined verb 'was' refers to the subject 'popularity', which is singular, thus 'was' is appropriate here.

   Past perfect tense 'had been' is incorrect for the sentence; Past perfect tense is needed when we refer to earlier of the two incidents in the past.

In option D, 'which' refers to masks, changing the meaning of the sentence; it does not refer to 'popularity'. Also, the use of "which clause" will turn the whole clause "was ....game" into a non-essential clause, leaving the sentence without a verb and creating a fragment.

For example:

· Right: Harvard is an excellent college. [A proper sentence]
· Wrong: Harvard, which is an excellent college. [Not a sentence, but a fragment]

The correct answer is A.

10. This is a question on the usage of pronouns.

Let us bring out the sentence, "*The popularity of Walt Disney cartoon figure Mickey Mouse masks was dependent on internalizing <u>its</u> use in children by making their presence part of a perceived game.*"

Option C is the correct answer because the underlined possessive pronoun refers to masks, which is plural, and "its" is meant for singular nouns; thus, 'their' meant for plural nouns is the correct answer.

Option D is incorrect as without 'their', there would be ambiguity, for whose 'use' the sentence refers to? 'Their' (possessive pronoun) has the noun 'masks' as the antecedent in the sentence.

Option B is incorrect because we need a pronoun; however, "there" is not a pronoun. "There" can be used to demonstrate (here and there) or can be used as a dummy subject in a sentence (there seems to be a problem), but "there" cannot be used as a pronoun.

The correct answer is C.

11. This is a question on grammatical construction.

Let us bring out the sentence, "*This camouflage potentially reduced the element of fear that the masks conveyed to their recipients.*"

Option A is the correct answer because the sentence '*This camouflage potentially reduced the element of fear that the masks conveyed to their recipients.*' correctly conveys the meaning. 'This camouflage' clearly refers to the adjustments being done to the masks, discussed in the previous sentences, adjustments that were done in order to avoid scaring the children and enhancing the use of the masks. The subject also links the sentence at hand with the previous sentence, providing an effective transition.

Option B is incorrect because it incorrectly means that the recipients conveyed the element of fear; however, the sentence means that the masks conveyed the element of fear, or rather could have conveyed fear had the masks not been tweaked to suit its use for children.

Option C is incorrect because it is awkwardly constructed and being is passive form, it lacks concision.

Option D is incorrect because it distorts the meaning of the sentence; it replaces 'elements of fear' with 'fear elements', creating meaning error.

The correct answer is A.

7.3   Passage 3: Sustainability of Homo Sapience

Passage 3

Sustainability of Homo Sapience

1. This is a question on the identification of redundancies.

   Let us bring out the sentence, "*The positioning of human beings as one of the species with the largest biomasses on earth, <u>and also as the leading influence</u> on earth's ecosystems ...*"

   Option C is the correct answer because it is free of any redundancies and conveys the correct meaning.

   Option A is incorrect because the words "and" and "also" mean the same thing; hence, they don't have to be used together.

   Option B is incorrect because it does not use an appropriate connector to join the two clauses. Using merely "also" is not enough to join the two phrases "as one ... earth" and "as the ... ecosystems"; a conjunction, in this case "and" is required to join the phrases.

   Option D is incorrect because it does not establish a grammatically correct sentence. The underlined part needs to form a proper continuation to "The positioning of human beings as"; however, "leading the influence" forms "the positioning of human beings as leading the influence" changes the meaning and is not parallel with the first half of the sentence that goes "the positioning of human beings as one of the species with the largest biomasses on earth."

   The correct answer is C.

2. This is question on the usage of prepositions.

   Let us bring out the sentence, "*The positioning of human beings as one of the species with the largest biomasses on earth, and also as the leading influence on earth's ecosystems is the result of the ecological processes which **brought** <u>upon</u> their migration from the African Savannah, and geographically dispersed them throughout the world.*"

   Option D is the correct answer because it provides the correct preposition, "about", in the context of this sentence.

   To mean "make something happen/resulted into", the correct idiom is "brought about", for example, the rains brought about (resulted into) the floods.

   "Brought upon" is not an idiom; it can be used only in the following manner – The criminals brought these hard times upon themselves. (Cause something)

   "Brought into" is to "produce/yield" and not "result in" – Stocks bring into risk to any portfolio.

   "Brought forth" means "to give rise to/give birth to" (to be used in descriptive, poetic sense, generally) – In the spring, plants bring forth fruits and flowers.

   The correct answer is D.

3. This is question on the usage of appropriate words - diction.

Let us bring out the sentence, "*Biomass is the total mass of all <u>lively</u> members of a species.*"

The sentence states that the total mass of all <adjective> members of a species. The word "lively" means "full of life (as a behavior);" however, the sentence, given its scientific discussion, does not intend to discuss the behavioral qualities of the members of species, but rather wishes to discuss biological characteristics; thus, biomass is the total mass of all members of a species that are alive. To mean so, the correct adjective is "living." So, option A is incorrect.

"Live" is an adjective, best used to discuss experiments, for example: the research was performed on live rats (not "living rats").

Also, use "live" for "animals" but "living" for human beings. So, option B is incorrect.

Option C is incorrect because while "alive" means "living", it is a postpositive adjective, as in, used not *before* the noun but *after* it; for example:

· Wrong: I found an alive kitten in the abandoned house.

· Right: I found a live kitten in the abandoned house.

· Right: The kitten is alive.

The correct answer is D.

4. This is question on the usage of pronouns.

Let us bring out the related sentences, "*It can be said that rudimentary measure of the success of the species is its position near the top of the aggregate biomass scale. Biomass is the total mass of all living members of a species. For human beings, <u>it</u> is a reflection of their claim on territory, and their consumption of resources as a species.*"

What is a reflection of their claim on territory? Human beings? Their biomass? No, <u>the fact that</u> their biomass is high enough to be near the top of the scale **is** a reflection of their claim on territory.

The intended meaning must be conveyed in a clear and crisp, non-ambiguous way. Sometimes when the subject of some verb is difficult to represent directly, placeholder pronouns are used. For example:

· It seems crazy that she left this lucrative job.

What seems crazy? That she left this lucrative job (The subject)

Thus, "it" is "holding place/representing" the subject "that she left this lucrative job".

Similarly, in the given sentence, we need a placeholder pronoun "it" to convey what exactly is a reflection of their claim on territory.

Option A is the correct answer because the sentence conveys the correct meaning as per the context by using the correct placeholder pronoun as no other option does.

Option B is incorrect because it uses "there." "There" is used as a placeholder subject only to indicate general presence of something; for example: There are four seasons in a year (general point). "There" cannot be used for actual, specific points or subjects: for example, it would be wrong to say "there seems crazy that she left this lucrative job."

Option C is incorrect because it incorrectly refers to human beings with "it" in "*its claim on territory*" and in "*consumption of resources by it as species*".

Option D is incorrect because it uses the plural form "reflections", whereas it should be singular, which goes against the context of the given sentence.

The correct answer is A.

5. This is question on the usage of transitional adverbs.

Let us bring out the related sentences, "*It might be short-sighted to belittle the success of an emerging species or breed for being small in number if it is evident that the members of the species are elegant and well-adjusted. Unfortunately, the ability to adapt one's habitat to the largest ecosystem, while still retaining the flexibility to deal with local demands on the population may be considered high art in the annals of successful adaptation.*"

The sentence before the transitional word "*It might be short-sighted . . . elegant and well-adjusted*" states that small numbers night not be a problem is the members are well-adjusted; the sentence after the transitional word states that any species that adapts to the largest ecosystem and still retains flexibility is even better at the art of adaptation. Thus, the sentence before the transitional word contrasts the sentence after the transitional word as the former implies that small numbers are good **but** large numbers with flexibility is even better. Thus, "however" is the best choice.

"Unfortunately" is out of context because the sentence implies positive fortune, not lack of it.

"Consequently" is used to discuss effects, not contrasts.

"Moreover" is used to give additional points about some previously introduced point, not for contrasts.

The correct answer is B.

6. This is a question on the comprehension of ideas.

Let us bring out the sentence, "*It is the fact that human beings have remained in a generally undifferentiated form that allows them to rank high as a single successful species.*"

Looking at the options, we find that option are distinguished on the usage of two words, one "*undifferentiated/differentiated*", used to describe humans and two, "*low/high*", used to describe rank.

From the context, we know that human species has largely remained undifferentiated i.e. unlike other species, it has not adapted by splitting into new species (inferable from the part that says "ability to adapt to the largest ecosystem (the earth) while still retaining the flexibility", implying that human beings have spread across the earth but still remained human beings and not become multiple, smaller, different species. Also, subsequent sentence "human beings are considered unique... environment" also attests to this). Referring to it with "undifferentiated" is correct, thus option B and D are ruled out.

Again from the first sentence of the passage, we know that among all species, human beings have the largest Biomass (except insects); thus, human species should be ranked high, and thus option A is correct.

The correct answer is A.

7. This is a question on comprehension.

Let us bring out the sentence, "*The whole world has been tenanted with life.*"

Option B is the correct answer because it shows the appropriate relation between 'world' and 'life'. "Life occupying/living in the world" makes the most logical sense here.

Options A, C and D are incorrect because they all show an illogical connection between "life" and "the world."

The correct answer is B.

8. This is a question on effective expressions.

   Let us bring out the sentence, "*Human beings are considered unique **as** they retain their forms **as** they travel from environment to environment*."

   Option B is the correct answer because it effectively shortens the sentence by removing the unnecessary "considered," and shortening the length by using "traversing," thereby avoiding the usage of the word "environment" twice.

   Option A is incorrect because it uses "as" twice in different meanings, making the sentence ambiguous.

   Option C is incorrect because it mentions "all environments," indicating the all human beings have travelled everywhere, changing the meaning drastically.

   Option D is incorrect because it has removed essential key words, leading to incomplete information. Also it illogically uses "uniform (same species)" instead of "unique (a unique species)" to describe human beings, creating a meaning error.

   The correct answer is B.

9. This is question on the usage of transition words.

   Let us bring out the related sentences, "*Historically, human beings, like all organisms, may be driven into new areas, or a new environment may spring up around them as a result of drought, competition or geological changes. Still, human beings have been able to adjust their behavior sufficiently to avoid having nature make such extensive piecemeal adjustments to them that entirely distinct workable alternatives of the same model occupy the new space.* "

   Option A is the correct answer because it correctly uses a conjunction "Still" to present a thought that is contrasting the thought mentioned in the previous sentence. The two sentences imply that human beings did face challenges to such an extent that they could have succumbed, **yet** they didn?t because they could adjust themselves well.

   Option B is incorrect because it indicates that the following sentence, "*… human beings have been able to adjust their behavior sufficiently to avoid having nature make such extensive piecemeal adjustments to them…*" is an alternate option, which is not.

   Option C in incorrect because it illogically indicates two things being compared; however, there is no such evidence found.

   Option D is incorrect because it raises the question of time or cause, neither of which is relevant in the given information in the passage.

   The correct answer is A.

10. This is a question on the expression of ideas.

    Let us bring out the sentence, "*Still, human beings have been able to adjust their behavior sufficiently to avoid having nature make such extensive piecemeal adjustments to them that entirely distinct workable alternatives of the same model occupy the new space.*" **10**

Option B is the correct answer because the additional information it provides usefully drives home the fact that humans haven't changed even though species around them have evolved over the years. Such information will bolster the point in the previous sentence very well, by providing proper illustrations.

Option A is incorrect because it mentions species in general, which can include human beings, thus changing the meaning.

Option C is incorrect because the illustration given is only mentioned after the satisfactory explanation, which is sufficient to not lead to any confusion.

Option D is incorrect because there is no need for an explanation of actual process of evolution.

The correct answer is B.

11. This is a question on the understanding of tables and graphs.

Option D is the correct answer because it is clearly shown in the graph that the marked areas for humans and that for domesticated animals have been steadily increasing from 1900 BC onwards and would achieve the largest growth by the year 2050. Comparatively, only wild animals are shown around 10000 BC and by 2050, they are shown to be the lowest segment.

Options A, B and C are all incorrect because they are wrong conclusions from the data given.

The correct answer is D.

7.4 Passage 4: Lord Dalhousie's reforms in india

Passage 4
Lord Dalhousie's reforms in india

1. This is a question on the usage of words and phrases.

   Let us bring out the sentence, "*The reforms introduced by Lord Dalhousie in India endangering his eight-year stint as the Governor General are many.*"

   Option D is the correct answer because it uses the correct preposition "during" to indicate that the reforms were only carried out in the time of Dalhousie's stay in India as seen from the next few sentences that follow "*Dalhousie introduced a new system of internal communication in India. Dalhousie convinced the authorities of the need of the railways and laid down the main lines of their development.*"

   Option A is incorrect because it incorrectly indicates that the reforms introduced by Dalhousie were putting him in some kind of trouble which is not in sync with what the passage indicates.

   Option B is incorrect because it is wrong to conclude that Dalhousie had introduced reforms as a prevention for something. Again the passage doesn't show any indicators for the same.

   Option C is incorrect because 'regarding' makes it seem that the reforms which Dalhousie introduced in India were about his eight-year stay there, which again is misleading.

   The correct answer is D.

2. This is a question on the usage of tenses.

   Let?s bring out the associated sentences, "*The reforms introduced by Lord Dalhousie in India during his eight-year stint as the Governor General are many. Dalhousie introduced a new system of internal communication in India. Dalhousie convinced the authorities of the need of the railways and laid down the main lines of their development.*"

   Option A is the correct answer. The tone of the passage (made obvious by the words, 'introduced' and 'convinced') is decidedly indicative of the fact that the reforms have been brought about in the past. Hence, the appropriate tense would be simple past tense which is what Option A indicates.

   Option B is incorrect because it incorrectly uses the future tense for describing something that has been already carried out.

   Option C and D both are incorrect because they use forms of present tense, which is incorrect in the given context.

   The correct answer is A.

3. This is question on the use of grammatical construction.

   Let us bring out the sentence, "*He envisaged a network of railways connecting the main places with the ports and providing both for strategic needs and commercial development.*"

Option A is incorrect because of the placement of 'both' in the sentence. It suggests that some two entities were provided for strategic needs and commercial development. Since the sentence doesn't talk of any two entities to which these were provided, this meaning is incorrect.

Option B is incorrect again for the placement of both. However, here it suggests that Dalhousie "envisaged a network of railways" for providing for strategic needs and commercial development and not that these two were a consequence of the spread of the railways.

Option C is incorrect because "providing for together" is grammatically incorrect in the given context.

Option D is the correct answer because it correctly places "both" after the preposition 'for' implying that 'both' refers to strategic needs and commercial development.

The correct answer is D.

4. This is a question on the expression of ideas.

   Let us bring out the sentence, *"Besides facilitating trade & commerce and minimizing distances, the railways have gone a long way in uniting India."*

   Option B is the correct answer because the sentence is clearly disconnected with the theme of the rest of the passage. While the rest of the passage talks of the various reforms introduced by Dalhousie (and hence, talks of the construction of railways in the process), the sentence in question focusses on the objectives of railways in the present times, which doesn't gel well with the remaining passage.

   Option A is incorrect because it provides an incorrect reason for deleting the underlined sentence. It is not because the sentence doesn't outline all the objectives of the railways equally, but because it talks of these objectives in the first place.

   Options C and D are incorrect because talking of "unification of India" being an objective, primary or otherwise, of the Indian Railways doesn't fit in the context of the passage.

   The correct answer is B.

5. This is a question on the usage of transition words.

   Let us bring out the related sentences, *"Besides facilitating trade and commerce, from the perspective of minimizing distances, the railways have gone a long way in uniting India. Nevertheless, in 1852 Dalhousie introduced the Electric Telegraph System in India."*

   Option B is the correct answer because the passage goes on to talk about another aspect of Dalhousie's impact on India which is about how he introduced the Electric Telegraph in India whereas the earlier part of the passage mentioned about him setting up the railways.

   Options A and C are incorrect because each word suggests a contrast which is not brought out by the contents of the statement in question.

   Option D is incorrect because it implies that Dalhousie set up the Telegraph system as a consequence of setting up of the railway system in India, whereas according to the passage both were independently undertaken by Dalhousie.

   The correct answer is B.

6. This is a question on subject-verb agreement.

   Option C is the correct answer because the singular verb 'was' agrees with the singular noun 'telegraph line' which appears in the sentence "*The first telegraph line was from Calcutta to Agra which were opened in 1854, and covered a distance of 800 miles.*"

   Options A and B are incorrect because the plural verbs "were" and "have" do not agree with the singular subject "telegraph".

   Option D is incorrect because it forms a run-on sentence.

   The correct answer is C.

7. This is a question on grammatical construction.

   Let us bring out the sentence, "*Hence working civilians were completely neglected by the military board.*"

   Option B is the correct answer because "*Public Works*" is mentioned in the previous sentence which also means "Civilian Works" as mentioned in this answer. It also provides reasoning for the forthcoming sentence, which says "*A separate Public Works Department was established by Lord Dalhousie.*"

   Option A is incorrect because it states 'working civilians' which indicates a different subject altogether.

   Option C is incorrect in saying civilians ignored the military board, which is a wrong correlation between the civilians and military board and incorrectly talks about civilians who weren't referred to by the writer at all.

   Option D is incorrect because it misunderstands 'Public Works' in the previous statement to be works of people and hence the entire meaning of the sentence changes.

   The correct answer is B.

8. This is a question on the usage of words.

   Let us bring out the sentence, "*Irrigational works were undertaken on an expensive scale.*"

   Option D is the correct answer because the preceding part of the given sentence talks about irrigation work being undertaken and goes on to say "*The construction of Ganges Canal was completed and was inaugurated on April 8, 1854. Many bridges and canals were constructed and the construction of Grand Trunk Road was also taken up.*" This clearly indicates that the work carried out on irrigation was expanding and all types of construction was being done for which 'extensive' is the most appropriate indicator.

   Option A is incorrect because it talks about monetary factor (expensive), which was not referred to in the rest of passage at all.

   Option B in incorrect because it would mean that the irrigation work wasn't carried out smoothly (erratic), something which is not indicated anywhere.

   Option C is incorrect because it incorrectly indicates that this type of irrigation work is carried out not only in India but everywhere else also in the world. Additionally, "universal?? doesn?t go with the article "an?? that precedes it and hence can be ruled out.

   The correct answer is D.

9. This is a question on the organization of ideas.

   Let us bring out the paragraph, *"[1] Nevertheless, in 1852 Dalhousie introduced the Electric Telegraph System in India. [2] The first telegraph line was from Calcutta to Agra which were opened in 1854, and covered a distance of 800 miles. [3] By 1857, it was extended to Lahore and Peshawar. [4] Before Lord Dalhousie, military boards were in charge of the construction of Public Works. Hence working civilians were completely neglected by the military board. [5] A separate Public Works Department was established by Lord Dalhousie. [6] Irrigational works were undertaken on an expensive scale. [7] The construction of Ganges Canal was completed and was inaugurated on April 8, 1854. [8] Many bridges and canals were constructed and the construction of Grand Trunk Road was also taken up. [9] Dalhousie's special contribution was the construction of an engineering college at Roorkee and in other presidencies."*

   Option A is the correct answer because before sentence 4, in statement 3 "*By 1857, it was extended to Lahore and Peshawar,*" 'it' refers to the telegraph system set up by Dalhousie. The two additional sentences also refer to the same system being extended.

   Options B, C, and D are all incorrect because they are all referring to locations after sentence 4, in which the writer starts talking about the neglect of Public Works by the military board which leads to a different subject altogether. The reference of the telegraph system is only before sentence 4.

   The correct answer is A.

10. This is a question on the usage of pronouns.

    Let us bring out the sentence, "*Dalhousie, who held many roles in the administration and internal development of the region, contributed to the Indian postal system doing away with <u>these past</u> obstructions and levying a uniform rate of postage.*"

    Option B is the correct answer because the 'obstructions?' mentioned in the sentence refers to the obstructions of "Indian postal system??" and 'its?' correctly refers to "Indian postal system??.

    Option A is incorrect because the use of the pronoun 'these?' suggests that the passage has already talked about some obstructions previously. This is clearly not the case.

    Option C is incorrect because the subject in this sentence is singular 'Indian postal system' and 'their' refers to a plural form for the noun.

    Option D is incorrect since no modifier before 'obstructions?' would make it ambiguous to the reader as to what these obstructions were and are in relation to what.

    The correct answer is B.

11. This is question on parallelism.

    Option D is the correct answer because "weight" and "charge" as per the given sentence "This idea of instituting a uniform unit of weighing and of charge for the whole of the vast Indian empire seemed sheer folly?" are nouns parallel to each other; they are units of measurement.

    Options A, B, and C are all incorrect because they are verbs, thus break parallelism.

    The correct answer is D.

7.5 Passage 5: Belgian economy

Passage 5
Belgian economy

1. This is a question on expression of ideas.

   Let us bring out the related sentences, "*For 200 years until World War I, French-speaking Wallonia was a technically advanced, industrial region. Consequently, Dutch-speaking Flanders was predominantly agricultural.*"

   Option B is the correct answer because the context suggests that Wallonia and Flanders were different in their economies, and the usage of the conjunction "while" here correctly brings out the contrast between the two clauses ("*French-speaking Wallonia was a technically advanced, industrial region*" and "*Dutch-speaking Flanders was predominantly agricultural.*").

   Option A is incorrect because it incorrectly implies that Flanders being predominantly agricultural is a result of Wallonia being technically advanced.

   Option C uses the phrase, "on the other hand," incorrectly. It should have been set off by commas on both sides to make for a grammatically correct sentence.

   Option D is incorrect because it introduces redundancy in the usage of the phrase "and at the same time" as the modifier "for 200 years until World War I" applies to both the clauses.

   The correct answer is B.

2. This is a question on the usage of adverbs.

   Let us bring out the sentence, "*The older, traditional industries of Wallonia, mostly steel-making, began to lose their competitive edge during this period, but the general growth of world prosperity masked this deterioration until the 1973 and 1979 oil price shocks and resultant shifts in international demand sent the economy into a period of prolonged recession.*"

   The sentence implies that the older, traditional industries were all losing their competitive edge but steelmaking bore the maximum brunt.

   Option C, "particularly" is the correct choice in this context.

   The adverb "mostly" means 'for greater part or number' or 'generally/usually'. Option A is incorrect because both these meanings of "mostly" do not fit into the context of the sentence.

   Options B and D are both adverbs that cannot precede the gerund (a form of noun) "steelmaking" in this case.

   The correct answer is C.

3. This is a question on grammatical construction.

   Let us bring out the sentence, "*The older, traditional industries of Wallonia, mostly steel-making, began to lose their competitive edge during this period, but the general growth of world prosperity masked this deterioration until the 1973 and 1979 oil price shocks and resultant shifts in international demand sent the economy into a period of prolonged recession.*"

Option A is the correct answer because it is the only choice that provides a grammatically standard and coherent sentence.

Option B is incorrect because it is wordy and imprecise and introduces repetition ("oil price shocks and resultant shifts. . . resulted in the economy. . . "). It also places the modifier "for prolonged periods" after "shifts in international demand" leading to a change in meaning.

Option C is incorrect because it uses the present tense ("lead") in a passage that is talking about events of the past.

Option D is incorrect because it leaves the sentence incomplete in the absence of a main verb for the last clause ("until the 1973 and 1979 oil price shocks and resultant shifts in international demand that led to a prolonged period of recession for the economy.")

The correct answer is A.

4. This is a question on usage of words and phrases.

Let us bring out the sentence, "*In the 1980s and 1990s, the economic center of the country continued to shift northwards to Flanders.*" It is clear from here that the geographical location of the economic center of Belgium gradually moved to Flanders.

Since this idea is best captured in the original phrase, option A is the correct answer.

Option B is incorrect because although "rise" can imply an upward movement, it doesn't fit in the context of the shift of a geographical location.

Option C is incorrect because the word "continued" suggests a gradual activity that keeps happening for some time, while "relocate" is a verb that is a discrete activity.

Option D is incorrect because the word "increase" doesn't fit in the context of a geographical location.

The correct answer is A.

5. This is a question on the expression of ideas.

Let us bring out the paragraph, "*[1] In the 1980s and 1990s, the economic center of the country continued to shift northwards to Flanders. [2] The early 1980s saw the country facing a difficult period of structural adjustment caused by declining demand for its traditional products, deteriorating economic performance, and neglected structural reform. [3] Against this grim backdrop, in 1982, Prime Minister Martens' center-right coalition government formulated an economic recovery program to promote export-led growth by enhancing the competitiveness of Belgium's export industries through an 8.5% devaluation. [4] Consequently, the 1980-82 recession shook Belgium to its core—unemployment rose, social welfare costs increased, personal debt was soaring, the government deficit climbed to 13% of GDP, and the national debt, although mostly held domestically, shrank. [5] Economic growth rose from 2% in 1984 to a peak of 4% in 1989. [6] In May 1990, the government linked the franc to the German Mark, primarily through closely tracking German interest rates.*"

The sentence 4 in question clearly states that the poor economic condition of Belgium is a "consequence" of 'something'. A careful reading of the paragraph suggests that it was in the light of a difficult period of structural adjustments that Belgium plunged into recession. Hence, it makes sense to talk about these consequences (recession, unemployment, etc.) after the cause for it has been highlighted (as in sentence 2).

Options A, B and D do not make for a coherent read and distort the flow of the passage.

The correct answer is C.

6. This is a question on parallelism.

   Let us bring out the sentence, "*Consequently, the 1980-82 recession shook Belgium to its core—unemployment rose, social welfare costs increased, <u>personal debt was soaring</u>, the government deficit climbed to 13% of GDP, and the national debt, although mostly held domestically, shrank.*"

   Option C is the correct answer because it is clear from the sentence structure that all the effects/consequences of the 1980-82 recession are listed in simple past tense, starting from "*unemployment rose*" to "*social welfare costs increased*" to "*government deficit climbed.*" Hence, by the rules of parallelism the underlined portion must also be in the simple past tense – "personal debt soared."

   The correct answer is C.

7. This is a question on usage of words and phrases.

   Let us bring out the sentence, "*Consequently, the 1980-82 recession shook Belgium to its core—unemployment rose, social welfare costs increased, personal debt soared, the government deficit climbed to 13% of GDP, and the national debt, although mostly held domestically, <u>shrank</u>.*"

   Option D is the correct answer because "mushroom" means to rapidly grow or increase in number, which goes perfectly for national debt.

   Options A and C are incorrect because "shrank" and "dwindle" both suggest to decrease in size, while the paragraph intends to suggest that national debt, like cost of social welfare and personal debt, increased manifold.

   Option B is incorrect because dilate means to become wider or more open, which doesn't fit in the context of increasing national debt.

   The correct answer is D.

8. This is a question on modifiers.

   Let us bring out the sentence, "*In May 1990, the government linked the franc to the German Mark, primarily through <u>closely tracking</u> German interest rates.*"

   Option A is the correct answer because "closely" is the adverb of manner that correctly modifies the verb "tracking" in the sentence.

   Options B and C are incorrect because "close tracking" and "close track" are noun phrases while the sentence requires a verb phrase.

   Option D incorrect because "close" incorrectly modifies "German interest rates" instead of the verb "tracking."

   The correct answer is A.

9. This is a question on the organization of ideas.

Let us bring out the paragraph, *"[1] In the 1980s and 1990s, the economic center of the country continued to shift northwards to Flanders. [2] The early 1980s saw the country facing a difficult period of structural adjustment caused by declining demand for its traditional products, deteriorating economic performance, and neglected structural reform. [3] Against this grim backdrop, in 1982, Prime Minister Martens' center-right coalition government formulated an economic recovery program to promote export-led growth by enhancing the competitiveness of Belgium's export industries through an 8.5% devaluation. [4] Consequently, the 1980-82 recession shook Belgium to its core—unemployment rose, social welfare costs increased, personal debt soared, the government deficit climbed to 13% of GDP, and the national debt, although mostly held domestically, mushroomed. [5] Economic growth rose from 2% in 1984 to a peak of 4% in 1989. [6] In May 1990, the government linked the franc to the German Mark, primarily through closely tracking German interest rates."*

Option B is the correct answer because sentence 3 talks about the consequences of "linking the franc with the German Mark" as is suggested in sentence 6. Hence, it makes sense to talk of the consequences of this policy on the Belgium economy after the policy has been talked about.

Options A, C and D are incorrect because the sentences preceding or succeeding the given options have no mention of the German interest rates.

The correct answer is B.

10. This is a question on punctuation.

Let us bring out the sentence, *"…and subsidized ailing industries; coal, steel, textiles, glass, and shipbuilding; in order to prop up the economy.*

The underlined part contains examples of industries to which workers were transferred.

Option B is the correct answer because it rightly sets off the list with em dashes (—) on both sides of the examples.

Options A and C are incorrect because any part after a semi colon in a sentence should be a complete clause, whereas in the given sentence it is only a list of industries.

Option D is incorrect because it breaks the sentence by introducing a period and leaving the next sentence incomplete.

The correct answer is B.

11. This is a question on expression of ideas.

Option C is the correct answer because the purpose of the sentence is to explain how owing to the high personal savings rate, some ill effects of the recession were minimized. Without this sentence, the following statement *"This minimized the deleterious effects on the overall economy."* loses its meaning.

Options D is incorrect because although the passage states that Belgium was a rich country, the given sentence is present in a different context altogether – it talks of the positive effects of the high personal savings rate in light of the prolonged recession that Belgium experienced.

The correct answer is C.

7.6   Passage 6: Accumulation of Oxygen

Passage 6
Accumulation of Oxygen

1. This is a question on tenses.

   Let us bring out the sentence, "*The earliest accumulation of oxygen in the atmosphere was arguably the most important biological event in Earth history.*"

   Option B is the correct answer because 'is arguably' is the correct tense. Since 'The earliest accumulation of oxygen in the atmosphere' is expected to remain the most important event for all times and does not stop being important now or in the future, simple present tense is used correctly.

   Option A is incorrect because 'was arguably' implies that the event is in the past and no more valid in the present.

   Option C is incorrect because 'being arguably' uses the incorrect form of the verb 'to be' here and produces an incomplete sentence too.

   Option D is incorrect because 'had been arguably' indicates that this action is time bound in the past and is not a generalization valid for posterity as suggested by the correct option B.

   The correct answer is B.

2. This is a question on verb and tenses.

   Let us bring out the sentence, "*A general consensus asserts that appreciable oxygen first accumulated in Earth's atmosphere around 2.3 billion years ago during the so-called Great Oxidation Event (GOE).*"

   Option A is the correct answer because the sentence is presented as a claim, thus it should be in simple present tense.

   Option B is incorrect because "assert (verb for plural)" does not agree with "consensus (singular)".

   As explained above, option C and D are incorrect because the sentence needs simple present tense.

   The correct answer is A.

3. This is a question on idiomatic usage.

   Let us bring out the sentence, "*Scientists have long speculated so as to why animal species didn't burgeon sooner even though plants have long started appearing and developing, once sufficient oxygen covered the Earth's surface.*"

   Option B is the correct answer because "as to" is the correct idiomatic connector. To join a dependent clause "why animal species . . ." to the main clause "Scientists have . . ." a connector is necessary.

   Option A is incorrect because "so as to" is not used to connect two clauses in such a manner. "So as to" means "in order to" It can be used in the in the following manner:

Mail your package on time so as to ensure its timely arrival. Insert "in order to" instead of "so as to" to judge whether it is correct.

Option C is incorrect because "as though" is used to introduce a hypothetical (subjunctive) clause, for example: She behaves as though she were the queen. The given sentence does not contain a hypothetical statement but contains a question.

Option D is incorrect because we need a proper connector to join the two clauses – the dependent to the main.

The correct answer is B.

4. This is a question on the usage of verb tenses.

   Let us look at the entire sentence: "*Scientists have long speculated as to why animal species didn't burgeon sooner even though plants <u>have long started</u> appearing and developing, once sufficient oxygen covered the Earth's surface.*"

   Option D is the correct answer because the past perfect tense is correctly used here – 'had long started' – to indicate that the action preceded the other verbs in the past tense – 'sufficient oxygen covered the Earth's surface' and "didn't burgeon."

   Past perfect tense is used to denote the earlier (or earliest) of two (or more) actions in past.

   Option A is incorrect since the present perfect tense is inappropriate in this sentence, as discussed above.

   Option B is incorrect because it uses the continuous verb form without any helping verb, creating an incomplete sentence or fragment.

   Option C is incorrect because the simple past tense used here gives the wrong impression that it occurred at the same point of time as the action 'sufficient oxygen covered the Earth's surface.'

The correct answer is D.

5. This is a question on organization of ideas.

   Let us bring out the paragraph, *[1] The earliest accumulation of oxygen in the atmosphere <u>is arguably</u> the most important biological event in Earth history. [2] A general consensus asserts that appreciable oxygen first accumulated in Earth's atmosphere around 2.3 billion years ago during the so-called Great Oxidation Event (GOE). [3] Scientists have long speculated as to why animal species didn't burgeon sooner even though plants <u>had long started</u> appearing and developing, once sufficient oxygen covered the Earth's surface. [4] Animals first appeared and began to prosper at the end of the Proterozoic period, about 600 to 700 million years ago—but the billion-year stretch before that, when there was also plenty of oxygen, there were no animals.*

   Sentence 2 '*A general consensus asserts that appreciable oxygen first accumulated in Earth's atmosphere around 2.3 billion years ago during the so-called Great Oxidation Event (GOE)*' talks about **general consensus about oxygen's accumulation for the first time**, and sentence 1 mentions the **earliest accumulation** of oxygen as the most important biological event in history, so it is logical to place sentence 2 where it is currently since it elaborates on the idea presented in sentence 1. Sentence 2 is also well followed by 3, which takes the 'general consensus' mentioned in sentence 2 and proceeds to the very specific 'scientists.'

Sentence 4 elaborates on the 'why animal species didn't burgeon sooner', talked in sentence 3 and hence both are well placed in the current organization. Sentence 5 resolves the paradox raised in sentence 4 and sentence 2 would be a digression if it is placed after sentence 4.

The correct answer is A.

6. This is a question on the usage of words and phrases.

   Let us bring out the related sentences, "*Evidently, the air was not oxygen-rich enough then. The oxygen levels during the billion or more years before raising animals were only 0.1 percent of what they are today.*"

   The second sentence means that the oxygen levels before the *evolution* of animals were 0.1 percent of what they are today. The underlined portion does mean 'the rise of animals' and not 'raising animals'. Mentioning 'raising animals' would incorrectly convey the meaning that *somebody* raised the animals instead of conveying that the animals evolved (by themselves).

   Option D is incorrect because like 'raising animals', 'the raise of animal' would also incorrectly convey the meaning as discussed above.

   The correct answer is B.

7. This is a question on ambiguity, verb and tense.

   Let us bring out the sentence, "*The oxygen levels during the billion or more years before the rise of animals were only 0.1 percent of what they are today.*"

   Option C is the correct answer because it unambiguously conveys the desired meaning.

   Option A, while correct in tenses, is incorrect because "they" is ambiguous: it could refer to "levels" or "animals"

   Option B is incorrect because it uses the singular pronoun "it" for the plural "levels".

   Option D is incorrect because it does not use either a pronoun or a noun to refer to "levels" as is necessary, since the comparison is between earlier and current levels.

   The correct answer is C.

8. This is a question of the usage of conjunctions.

   Let us bring out the sentence, "*Since there is no question that genetic and ecological innovations are ultimately behind the rise of animals, there is also no question that for animal life to flourish, a certain level of oxygen is required.*"

   The usage of transition word 'Since' implies that the two parts of the sentence has cause and effect relationship; however, it is not so.

   The first clause "*there is no question that genetic and ecological innovations are ultimately behind the rise of animals*" asserts that genetic and ecological innovations are ultimately behind the rise of animals, and the second clause "*there is also no question that for animal life to flourish, a certain level of oxygen is required*" asserts that for animal life to flourish, a certain level of oxygen is required. Thus, the relation is of acknowledging a certain point **but** stating that something else is also to be considered. Thus, we need a conjunction that conveys the contrast but not too strong a contrast. "While" is ideal for this requirement, because it is a contrast conjunction, slightly contrasting, and also incorporates that some point can be conceding. For example: While you are right in what you think, I am not wrong in what I think.

"While" conveys the ideal transition of "agreed but, at the same time...".

["While" can also be used to indicate simultaneous actions – While walking, I was talking on the phone.]

'If' is incorrect because it is used to indicate conditions with results.

'Despite' is not a conjunction and thus cannot be used to join two clauses.

The correct answer is B.

9. This is a question on organization of idea.

   Let us bring out the related sentences, "*While there is no question that genetic and eco-logical innovations are ultimately behind the rise of animals, there is also no question that for animal life to flourish, a certain level of oxygen is required. The evidence was found by analyzing chromium isotopes in ancient sediments from China, Australia, Canada, and the United States. Chromium is found in the Earth's continental crust, and chromium oxi-dation, the process recorded by the chromium isotopes, are directly linked to the presence of free oxygen in the atmosphere.*"

   We see that the sentence before the underlined sentence talks about the importance of oxygen. The underlined sentence talks about the evidence of availability of oxygen, sources, and countries. The sentence that follows the underlined sentence refers to 'Chromium,' which is mentioned in the underlined sentence. Thus in order to present the idea cohesively, the underlined sentence must be kept.

   Option A is incorrect because the underlined sentence does not provide a detail that supports the main topic of the paragraph—**The earliest accumulation of oxygen in the atmosphere**—it rather presents a fact based on which the rest of the paragraph follows.

   The correct answer is B.

10. This is a question of usage of verbs and agreement.

    Let us bring out the sentence, "*Chromium is found in the Earth's continental crust, and chromium oxidation, the process recorded by the chromium isotopes are directly linked to the presence of free oxygen in the atmosphere.*"

    Option D is the correct answer because the underlined portion refers to the 'process', which is singular, thus 'is directly linked' is the correct usage.

    Option B is incorrect because it will form a fragment or an incomplete sentence.

    Option C is incorrect because the sentence is a factual statement; using 'has been linked' will ambiguously imply that the process recorded by the chromium isotopes might not be directly linked to the presence of free oxygen in the atmosphere **now**.

    The correct answer is D.

11. This is a question on grammatical construction.

    Let us bring out the sentence, "*Specifically, samples were deposited near the ancient shore-line in shallow, iron-rich ocean areas were studied...*"

    Option D is the correct answer because "samples" is the subject and "were studied" is its verb whereas "deposited...areas" is meant as an essential modifier for "samples". Modi-fier cannot contain functional verbs. If we add "were" to the modifier "deposited...areas", the verb "were studied" will be left without a subject, making the sentence insupportable and illogical. Same would be the case if any other verb were added.

The correct answer is D.

7.7   Passage 7: Fast food and obesity

Passage 7
Fast food and obesity

1. This is a question on redundancy.

   Let us bring out the sentence, "*Studies show that <u>obesity is increasing rapidly across</u> all age groups.*"

   Option B is the correct answer because "very" is redundant here. The phrase "*obesity is increasing rapidly across*" itself is sufficient to convey the meaning that obesity is increasing rapidly across all age groups.

   All the other options are grammatically correct and can effectively replace the underlined phrase to convey the desired meaning.

   The correct answer is B.

2. This is a question on the usage of verb and tenses.

   Let us bring out the sentence, "*The proposed conclusions contend that the brains of <u>overeaters experienced chemical changes</u> in response to unbalanced diets with a high content of processed sugar, salt, and saturated fats.*"

   Option B is the correct answer because the sentence presents a fact as a conclusion, thus it must be in present tense.

   All general observations, results of experiments, and universal truths must be presented in simple present tense.

   For example:

   · Right: The sun rises in the East.
   · Wrong: The sun rose in the East.
   · Right: We have observed that frogs always croak during monsoons.
   · Wrong: We have observed that frogs always croaked during monsoons.

   Option A and C are incorrect because they are written in past tenses, breaking the rule stated above and implying that the observation might not hold true anymore, i.e. "overeaters do not experience chemical changes anymore; they did so only in the past".

   Option D is incorrect because it is a fragment and not a complete sentence. To effectively communicate the idea, the verb "experience" needs an object, which is missing if we turn the object "chemical changes" into adverb and verb "chemically changed".

   The correct answer is B.

3. This is a question on the usage of pronouns.

   Let us bring out the sentence, "*It is a view that is increasingly supported by scientists who see a co-dependency between people's decisions and environmental influences (including the wide availability of people's favorite "fast foods") <u>that have structural effects</u> on human development.*"

Option A is the correct answer because the dependent clause "that have structural effects on human development" modifies "environmental influences", which is plural, thus option D is ruled out.

The relative pronoun 'who' can modify only people. Though either 'that' or 'which' can refer to "environmental influences", option C replaces 'effects' with 'affects', bringing in an error in diction. "Influences" in this context is a noun and can be replaced only by the noun "effects" and not by the verb "affects".

The correct answer is A.

4. This is a question on organization of ideas.

   Option D is the correct answer because sentence 3 is a conclusion of the paragraph, so the best place for it is at the end of that paragraph.

   It is logical to talk about chemical changes in brain in response to unbalanced diets after discussing evidence from scientists and researchers' findings.

   The correct answer is D.

5. This is a question on the usage of pronoun agreement and diction.

   Let us bring out the sentence, "*In time and in some cases, if people continue a pattern of consumption containing too much unhealthy food, their intake of this food will initiate changes in the brain that elevates the minimum level of ingestion the brain needs for satiation.*"

   Option A is the correct answer because "their" correctly refers to "people" and "this food" correctly refers to "unhealthy food."

   Option B and D are incorrect because the noun "intakes" is not standard, acceptable English. As a noun "intake" is always singular, regardless of number of people being discussed. As a verb "intake" will be conjugated according to the subject.

   Also, plural "these foods" will be incorrect to refer to the singular "unhealthy food."

   Option C is incorrect because "its" (pronoun meant for singular, non-people nouns) incorrectly refers to "people" (a plural noun).

   The correct answer is A.

6. This is a question on modifiers.

   Let us bring out the sentence, "*In time and in some cases, if people continue a pattern of consumption containing too much unhealthy food, their intake of this food will initiate changes in the brain that elevates the minimum level of ingestion the brain needs for satiation.*"

   Option B is the correct answer because currently the sentence "*… intake of this food will initiate changes in the brain that elevates the minimum level of ingestion…*" incorrectly means that when people eat too much unhealthy food, the brain will change and the changed brain will elevate the minimum satiety level. However, this meaning is incorrect because, if the sentence wished to indicate a sequential cause and effect chain, it would have said "if people… initiate changes in the brain that, *in turn*, elevates…" The sentence is actually implying that when people eat too much unhealthy food, changes happen in the brain, and as a result of this whole sequence, minimum satiety levels get elevated. Thus, the "elevation" is a consequence of the previous sentence, a modifier for the entire

sentence. So, we need to use an absolute phrase in the following manner: "if people...
changes in the brain, elevating the minimum..."

The correct answer is B.

7. This is a question on effective expressions.

Let us bring out the sentence, "*..., large, recurrent doses of "fast food" can* <u>*mimic the*</u>
<u>*effects*</u> *of opiates ,...."*

The implied meaning of the sentence is that big and regular intakes of fast food can do
what opium does to brains. It implies that fast foods can also play the role of opiates to
some extent.

Option B is the correct answer because after replacing it in the sentence "*...*, *large,*
recurrent doses of "fast food" can <u>*play the role*</u> *of opiates ,...."*, the meaning is conveyed
without compromise. In this case, "mimic" is used in its natural meaning – that is, to
duplicate, simulate, etc. Thus, "play the role" works as a perfect replacement of "mimic
the effects"

Option A is incorrect because the sentence does not intend to mean "ill-effects of opiates"
nor can "replace" work instead of "mimic".

Option C is incorrect because the sentence does not intend to mean "alleviate (lessen) the
effect of opiates".

Option D is incorrect because the sentence does not intend to mean "eliminate the effect
of opiates".

The correct answer is B.

8. This is a question on the expression of ideas.

Let us bring out the sentence, "*Scientists raising rats on a diet of twenty-five percent sugar*
found that upon suddenly eliminating glucose from the rats' food supply, the animals
experienced all the symptoms of withdrawal attributed to reducing traditional addictive
opiates, including shivering and chattering teeth."

Option C is the correct answer because the purpose of the sentence is to draw a parallel
between humans and rats. By citing the experiment on rats, scientist wished to drive a
point that if the symptoms can occur with rats, so can the symptoms with humans.

Moreover, the sentences followed by this talks more about the experiment on rats, making the sentence necessary.

Option D is incorrect because the passage does not suggest anything of this sort.

The correct answer is C.

9. This is a question on comparison.

Let us bring out the sentence, "*By this reasoning, obesity,* <u>*like*</u> *other addictions, can be*
viewed as a disease beyond the control of those afflicted by it."

The sentence compares two things – obesity and other addictions and intends to mean
that these two things are alike in a certain characteristic.

Option A is the correct answer because "like" correctly compares obesity and other addictions; moreover, to compare two nouns, "like" is used.

Option B is incorrect because "unlike" illogically presents a contrast between the two –obesity and other addictions. If obesity and other addictions were different, the paragraph would not have drawn similarities between overeating and opiates or used the phrase "by this reasoning."

Option C is incorrect because "as" is not used to compare two nouns; it is applied to compare two actions. Example: The current generation *wants to own* a house, *as did* the earlier generation.

Option D is incorrect because "such as" is used to cite examples and in the context it is irrelevant.

The correct answer is A.

10. This is a question on parallelism.

Let us bring out the sentence, "*This has brought lawyers to argue that civil society has a responsibility to regulate food <u>and educating people</u> about the abuse of "unhealthy foods" in a way that is comparable to society's control of opiates and narcotics.*"

Option C is the correct answer because "regulate people" and "educate people" are parallel. Items joined by conjunctions (and) must be made parallel.

Option A is incorrect because "... has a responsibility *to regulate* food and *educating people*" are not parallel.

Option D is incorrect because connecting "educate people" with "hence" is illogical; "educate people" is not the consequence of "regulate people". For the same reason, option B is also incorrect.

The correct answer is C.

11. This is a question on the organization of ideas.

Let us bring out the paragraph, "*[1] This has brought lawyers to argue that civil society has a responsibility to regulate food and educate people about the abuse of "unhealthy foods" in a way that is comparable to society's control of opiates and narcotics. [2] Corporations that target this vulnerability in human beings can then be held liable for the sicknesses that result from the poor eating habits overwhelming their customers. [3] For these researchers, the distinction between a habit and an addiction is not quantitative but qualitative. [4] Their consensus is that individuals can still moderate their behavior to control the effects of what they eat on their systems.*" **11**

Option C is the correct answer because the sentence 3 starts with "For these researchers, . . .", and <u>these researchers</u> does not have any reference in the paragraph, and thus, the best place for suggested statement—which talks about scientists' opinion—is before sentence 3. The scientists can be referred to as researchers. Also, the "still" provides the requisite contrast from sentences 1 and 2 to sentences 3 and 4. Sentences 1 and 2 talk in favor of regulations whereas sentences 3 and 4 suggest that instead of the corporations, the individuals must regulate their behavior. This contrast can be shown by "still".

The correct answer is C.

7.8   Passage 8: In-fighting princes

Passage 8
In-fighting princes

1. This is a question on the usage of phrases.

   Let us bring out the sentence, *"For 17th century Europeans, the history of Eastern monarchies, <u>such as</u> everything else in Asia, was stereotyped and invariable."*

   While 'like' implies comparison, 'such as' is used to list/introduce examples of the type or person you have just mentioned.

   Option B is the correct answer because in this context the sentence implies comparison and is not listing down examples.

   Option C is incorrect because 'similar as' is an incorrect idiomatic expression. 'Similar to' is the correct phrase.

   Option D is incorrect because the sentence only intends to imply similarity and not exactness. 'Same as' is incorrect in the given context.

   The correct answer is B.

2. This is a question on expression of ideas.

   Let us bring out the sentence, *"According to similar typical accounts of Indian events, history <u>displayed itself as</u> the predictable rituals of heavy-handed folklore."*

   The sentence here implies that history played out in a predictable fashion – being full of inconsiderate and insensitive activities.

   Option C is the correct answer because "unfolded itself" rightly implies to 'happen or to develop'.

   Options A and D are incorrect because both 'displayed itself as' and 'folded' within itself' are grammatically incorrect when used to describe history.

   Option B is incorrect because the passage nowhere suggests that the history was repeating itself; it only meant that whatever was happening was predictable.

   The correct answer is C.

3. This is a question on usage of words and phrases.

   Let us bring out the sentence, *"Typically, the founder of a dynasty, a brave soldier, is a desperate intriguer, and <u>expels from the throne</u> the feeble and degenerate scions of a more ancient house."*

   Option A is the correct answer because it rightly expresses the meaning of the sentence while being grammatically correct within the given sentence.

   Option B is incorrect because "evacuate" is incorrect to be used in the context of a throne.

   Option C is incorrect because "dethrones from the throne" introduces redundancy as "from the throne" is implicit in the verb "dethrone".

Option D is incorrect because one doesn't "uproot" someone from the throne – one can remove or dethrone someone.

The correct answer is A.

4. This is a question on subject verb agreement.

   Let us bring out the sentence, "*This founder's son may inherit some of the talent of the father; but in two or three generations luxury and indolence <u>does its</u> work, and the feeble inheritors of a great name are dethroned by some new adventurer, destined to bequeath a like misfortune to his degenerate descendants.*"

   It is clear from the sentence that subject for the verb 'do' in this case is "luxury and indolence". Since the subject is plural in number, it should be followed by a plural verb (do) and plural pronoun (their).

   Option D is the correct answer because it contains the right verb and pronoun that go with the plural subject "luxury and indolence".

   The correct answer is D.

5. This is a question on the usage of punctuation.

   Let us bring out the related sentences, "*This founder's son may inherit some of the talent of the father; but in two or three generations luxury and indolence do their work, and the feeble inheritors of a great name are dethroned by some new adventurer, destined to bequeath a like misfortune to his degenerate <u>descendants. Thus</u> rebellion and deposition were the correctives of despotism, and therefore, a recurrence, at fixed intervals, of able and vigorous princes through the medium of periodical anarchy and civil war, occurred.*"

   Option B is the correct answer because it provides the correct punctuation for the sentence that begins with "thus" (being used as a transition marker here) which implies that what follows is a result of the fact that you have just mentioned. "Thus", when used in beginning of a sentence is usually followed by a comma.

   Option A is incorrect because it leaves out the important comma that should follow "thus".

   Options C and D are incorrect because they both drop the period between the two sentences and unnecessarily elongating the already complex sentence. Moreover, the previous sentence already uses a semi colon and another clause after a semi colon will only make the sentence awkward.

   The correct answer is B.

6. This is a question on parallelism.

   Let us bring out the related sentence, "*Thus, rebellion and deposition were the correctives of despotism, and therefore, a recurrence, at fixed intervals, of able and vigorous princes through the medium of periodical anarchy and civil war, <u>was occurring</u>.*"

   On carefully reading the complete passage and this sentence in particular, one can easily infer that events of the past are being recounted. However, the underlined part suggests continuous tense, while the remaining sentence is given in simple past tense. This makes the sentence lose its parallel structure.

   Option D is the correct answer because according to the rules of parallelism, for events referring to same time frame, the same tense should be used throughout in the sentence. Hence, the sentence requires simple past tense.

The correct answer is D.

7. This is a question on grammatical construction.

   Let us bring out the sentence, *"It was this perception of history that allowed Britain's rulers to lie claim to the governance of the subcontinent."*

   Lie and lay, as verbs, are often confused words. While "lie" means to recline, "lay" means to place something, to put something on something.

   Option B is the correct answer because the context here demands the use of "lay" – to place claim over something or "to lay claim".

   Options C and D are incorrect because they use the incorrect tense form of the verb "lay".

   The correct answer is B.

8. This is a question on organization of ideas.

   Let us bring out the related sentences, *"[5] Thus, rebellion and deposition were the correctives of despotism, and therefore, a recurrence, at fixed intervals, of able and vigorous princes through the medium of periodical anarchy and civil war, was occurring. [6] It was this perception of history that allowed Britain's rulers to lay claim to the governance of the subcontinent. [7] This claim justified British policy, as well as dictated how they thought about gaining the favor of India's local monarchies. [8] The rationale that justified their actions to the British public was that avoiding such upheaval to allow peaceful reign over India was their ultimate goal. [9] The British claimed to be interested in avoiding these periods of bloodshed."*

   Option C is the correct answer because on reading the paragraph carefully, we can understand that the claim being talked about in sentence 7 is the Britain's claim "to be interested in avoiding these periods of bloodshed," mentioned in sentence 9. Hence, the logical position for sentence 9 is before sentence 7. ("This claim" in sentence 7 should come after the claim has been described.)

   Option A is incorrect because the sentence at the end of the paragraph seems disjoint after the related discussion is over.

   Option D is incorrect because it doesn't make sense to talk of the reasons/excuses that the British gave to their people before mentioning that they were ruling the subcontinent.

   The correct answer is C.

9. This is a question on the usage of words and phrases.

   Let us bring out the sentence, *"British armies and British administrators were able to insinuate rule over India by two primary methods."*

   Insinuate, in the given context, means to maneuver oneself into (a favorable position) by subtle manipulation.

   Option A is the correct answer because the sentence seeks to state that the British were able to maneuver themselves into a ruling position by the use of two methods. Insinuate fits in well in this context.

   Option B is incorrect because "tried to enter into rule over" is grammatically incorrect.

   Options C and D are incorrect because "were able to enjoy" and "monopolized their rule" do not fit in the context of the sentence as the sentence only talks about establishing rule, which logically precedes enjoying or monopolizing (an established) rule.

The correct answer is A.

10. This is a question on the usage of punctuation.

Let us bring out the sentence, "*By the Doctrine of Lapse, if the king of a subordinate state died without a natural male heir, then the kingdom would 'lapse' to the <u>British i.e.</u> it would automatically pass into the hands of the British.*"

The underlined portion has the abbreviation "i.e." (*id est*) which is Latin for 'that is'. Note that both 'i' and 'e' are followed by periods and the abbreviation is always preceded and followed by a comma. The same is also true for e.g., which stands for 'for example'.

Option D is the correct answer because it provides the correct punctuation for the given abbreviation.

The correct answer is D.

11. This is a question on the organization of ideas.

Let us bring out the related sentences, "*[1] British armies and British administrators were able to insinuate rule over India by two primary methods. [2] The first of these was the outright annexation of Indian states and subsequent direct governance of the underlying regions. [3] The second form of asserting power involved treaties in which Indian rulers acknowledged the Company's hegemony in return for limited internal autonomy. [4] The most important such support came from the subsidiary alliances with Indian princes during the first 75 years of Company rule. [5] The British achieved this by setting up native princes in positions of power. [6] Their methods took advantage of existing "doctrines of lapse", and made use of what was already the declared law in cases of heredity.*"

Option D is the correct answer because sentence 4 which starts with "The most important such support..." Note that "such support" doesn't find an antecedent in the paragraph. However, the new sentence talks of the need ("*support*") to set up political underpinnings given the financial constraints. It is hence logical to place this new sentence before sentence 4 because it provides the much needed antecedent for the phrase "such support" and makes complete sense in the given context.

The correct answer is D.

7.9   Passage 9: Abortion Law

Passage 9
Abortion Law

1. This is a question on the usage of words.

   Let us bring out the related paragraph *"The question of legalized abortion in America has largely been considered in terms of moral objections resulting from* <u>*compelling perceptions*</u> *of human rights and freedom of choice. While the representatives of these views have been influential actors for whom lawmakers must tweak any legislation pertains with abortion, economists now offer tangible evidence that the abortion issue must be evaluated with some very practical considerations as well. Inasmuch as the importance of the life of a foetus brought-to-term is never a forgotten aspect of the debate on abortion, the relevance of the abortion issue to the lifestyle opportunities for all of society has yet to be weighed heavily in the debate."*

   Option D is the correct answer because 'competing perceptions' means multiple perceptions that are competing with each other for supremacy. This usage goes hand-in-glove with the words 'the question of legalized abortion' in the first sentence and the 'while' constructions bringing out contrast in sentence.

   Option A is incorrect because 'compelling perceptions' which means 'perceptions that evoke interest' would not befit this context.

   Option B is incorrect because 'competitive perceptions' which means 'perceptions where competition is an essential element' would not befit this context.

   Option C is incorrect because 'complementary perceptions' which means 'perceptions that combine in such a way as to enhance or emphasize the qualities of each other' would not befit this context.

   The correct answer is D.

2. This is a question on verb form and prepositions.

   Let us bring out the sentence *"While the representatives of these views have been influential actors for whom lawmakers must tweak any legislation* <u>*pertains with*</u> *abortion, economists now offer tangible evidence that the abortion issue must be evaluated with some very practical considerations as well."*

   Option C is the correct answer because the gerund form 'pertaining' is correctly used here instead of the verb form 'pertains.' Moreover, 'to' is the correct preposition to be placed after 'pertain.'

   Option B is incorrect because 'pertains' would incorrectly make 'legislation' the subject in the sentence instead of the object. Moreover, 'with' is an incorrect preposition here.

   Option D is incorrect because 'with' is the incorrect preposition to follow 'pertain.'

   The correct answer is C.

3. This is a question on sentence structure.

   Let us bring out the sentence, *"Inasmuch as the importance of the life of a foetus brought-to-term is never a forgotten aspect of the debate on abortion, the relevance of the abortion issue to the lifestyle opportunities for all of society has yet to be weighed heavily in the debate."*

   Option B is the correct answer because 'while' is an appropriate structural word for a sentence that is expressing two contrasting ideas.

   Option A is incorrect because 'inasmuch as' is appropriate either to indicate a cause-effect relationship or to show extent.

   Option C is incorrect because 'since' is appropriate either to indicate a cause-effect relationship or to express a time relationship.

   Option D is incorrect because 'however' is an appropriate transition word to indicate a contrasting idea with that expressed in the preceding statement/s.

   The correct answer is B.

4. This is a question on verb form and tense.

   Let us bring out the sentence, *"However, in their retrospective examination of many years' evidence, John Donahue and Steven Levitt, researchers from Harvard University and the University of Chicago, pointing out that a suggested correlation between the passage of Roe vs. Wade, the integral piece of abortion empowerment legislation, and reported crime statistics twenty years later can in fact be noted."*

   Option D is the correct answer because 'have pointed' is an appropriate tense in this context and also creates a complete sentence and not a fragment as would be created by 'pointing.'

   Option B is incorrect because the present continuous tense 'are pointing' indicates that an action is occurring in the present moment. This is inappropriate in this context.

   Option C is incorrect because the past perfect tense 'had pointed' indicates that this verb preceded another verb in the past tense in the same sentence. However, this sentence does not contain any such reference to a past tense.

   The correct answer is D.

5. This is a question on tenses.

   Let us bring out the related sentences *"The researchers note that children who had otherwise been born in the early years after the Roe vs. Wade decision would be reaching their late teen years between 1985 and 1997. However, they were not born, therefore crime decreased in this time frame"*

   Option B is the correct answer because 'would have otherwise been' is appropriately used to indicate a hypothetical situation, as indicated by the next sentence (However, they were not born) and by the words 'otherwise' and 'would be reaching.'

   Options A, C, and D are incorrect because 'had otherwise been,' 'have otherwise been,' and 'were otherwise' indicate that this action actually occurred, and would render the sentence meaningless.

   The correct answer is B.

6. This is a question on conjunctions.

   Let us bring out the sentence, *"However, they were not born, __therefore__ crime decreased in this time frame."*

   Option D is the correct answer because 'so' is a Coordinating Conjunction, which is correctly used to join two independent clauses.

   Options A, B, and C are incorrect because 'therefore,' 'thus,' and 'hence,' although correctly indicate a cause-effect relationship, cannot be used to join two independent clauses. The only valid conjunctions that can join two individual clauses are indicated by the acronym FANBOYS: for, and, nor, but, or, yet, so.

   The correct answer is D.

7. This is a question on idiomatic usage and concision.

   Let us bring out the sentence, *"These researchers interpret the termination of an unwanted pregnancy as the rational response of a woman who is not prepared to __provide care for__ a child."*

   Option B is the correct answer because 'care for' means 'look after and provide for the needs of' and is a concise form of 'provide care for.'

   Option C is incorrect because 'care about' would indicate 'hold something dear,' and is incorrect in the context.

   Option D is incorrect because "not prepared to 'care less for'" is a double negative and would mean 'prepared to care for,' not fitting the context.

   The correct answer is B.

8. This is a question on sentence structure.

   Let us bring out the sentence, *"Going forward with an unwanted pregnancy presumably confers on the woman too great a challenge in raising a child she is poorly prepared __for, providing__ the child with an upbringing where is suboptimal, making him more vulnerable to be party to illegal conduct."*

   Option C is the correct answer because 'for, and provides' correctly uses 'and,' ensuring that the subject for the verb 'provides' is 'Going forward with an unwanted pregnancy' instead of 'providing' which confers a cause-effect relationship, rendering the sentence meaningless.

   Option B is incorrect because 'for; and provides' creates a sentence fragment (a missing subject in this case).

   Option D is incorrect because 'for, and providing' is not parallel construction and an incorrect verb form.

   The correct answer is C.

9. This is a question on conjunctions.

   Let us bring out the sentence, *"Going forward with an unwanted pregnancy presumably confers on the woman too great a challenge in raising a child she is poorly prepared for, and provides the child with an upbringing __where__ is suboptimal, making him more vulnerable to be party to illegal conduct."*

Option D is the correct answer because 'upbringing' is an abstract noun and can only be modified with 'that' or 'which.' 'That' is aptly restricting/defining the word upbringing. 'Which' is non-restrictive and 'upbringing which is suboptimal' does not restrict the meaning as does 'upbringing that is suboptimal.'

Option A is incorrect because 'where' indicates place and is inappropriately modifying 'upbringing.'

Option B is incorrect because 'when' indicates time and is inappropriately modifying 'upbringing.'

The correct answer is D.

10. This is a question on preposition.

Let us bring out the sentence, *"As the ideological <u>arguments of</u> abortion refuse to abate, it may be time for hamstrung legislators to consider new sources of information to simplify their decisions about reopening the question of abortion reform and government aid."*

Option C is the correct answer because 'arguments over' is the correct prepositional usage, not 'arguments of.'

OptionsBand D are incorrect because the passage talks about both support for and against abortion, so neither 'for' nor 'against' will be correct by itself.

The correct answer is C.

11. This is a question on expression of ideas.

Let us bring out the related sentences, *"[1] These numbers signify less crime as a result of letting more mothers choose when to have a baby. [2] Crime is financially costly to taxpayers as well. [3] As the ideological arguments over abortion refuse to abate, it may be time for hamstrung legislators to consider new sources of information to simplify their decisions about reopening the question of abortion reform and government aid."* **11**

Option C is the correct answer because the suggested sentence talks about the 'economic benefit to society from the termination of unwanted pregnancies' and is building on the idea expressed in sentence 2 "Crime is financially costly to taxpayers as well."

Options A, B and D are incorrect as they would create an incoherent paragraph.

The correct answer is C.

7.10   Passage 10: Proteins Therapeutics

Passage 10
Proteins Therapeutics

1. This is a question on modifiers.

    Let us bring out the sentence, "*Once a rarely used subset of medical treatments, <u>the use of protein therapeutics has</u> increased dramatically in number and frequency of use since the introduction of the first recombinant protein therapeutic–human insulin–25 years ago.*"

    Option B is the correct answer because the description or modifier 'once a rarely used subset of medical treatments' refers to the subject 'protein therapeutics,' and this subject must be placed unambiguously close to the modifier: immediately after the comma.

    Options A, C, and D are incorrect because none refer to 'protein therapeutics'; they either refer to protein therapeutics' usage or its importance.

    The correct answer is B.

2. This is a question on usage of punctuation.

    Let us bring out the sentence, "*Once a rarely used subset of medical treatments, protein therapeutics have increased dramatically in number and frequency of use since the introduction of the first recombinant <u>protein therapeutic–human insuin–25 years ago.</u>*"

    Option A is the correct answer because a non-essential modifier, here, *human insulin*, must be within a comma pair or a pair of dashes. Thus, option C is incorrect.

    Option B is incorrect because a semi-colon is used to join two independent clauses, which is not the case here.

    The correct answer is A.

3. This is a question on Sentence structure.

    Let us bring out the sentence, "*Protein therapeutics already have a significant role in almost every field of medicine <u>but</u> this role is still only in its infancy.*"

    Option B is the correct answer because two independent clauses can be joined by FAN-BOYS conjunctions, here, *but,* preceded with commas. Thus, options A and D are incorrect.

    Option C is incorrect because 'however', a transitional conjunction, should be preceded by a semi-colon or if the usage implies strong transition, it may be preceded by a period.

    The correct answer is B.

4. This is a question on usage of word.

    Let us bring out the sentence, "*Human proteins, <u>such as</u> erythropoietin, granulocyte colony–stimulating factor and alpha-L-iduronidase, are in great demand for the treatment of a variety of diseases.*"

    Option A is the correct answer because 'such as' is used to introduce examples, and erythropoietin, granulocyte colony–stimulating factor and alpha-L-iduronidase are specific examples of human proteins.

Option B is incorrect because 'like' is used to compare or tell about similarities. As stated that erythropoietin, granulocyte colony–stimulating factor and alpha-L-iduronidase are specific examples of human proteins and the context does not intend to mean that Human proteins, like [following types:] erythropoietin, granulocyte colony–stimulating factor and alpha-L-iduronidase, are in great demand...

Option C and D are incorrect because 'such as like' and 'like as' are incorrect idiomatic usage.

The correct answer is A.

5. This is a question on the usage of transition words.

   Let us bring out the sentence, "*Some can be purified from <u>blood, this</u> is expensive and runs the risk of contamination by AIDS or hepatitis C.*"

   Option C is the correct answer because the sentence means that some [proteins] can be purified from blood, [but] this [process] is expensive and runs the risk of contamination... This presents a contrast, thus either 'but' or 'however' should be used.

   Option A is incorrect because it creates a run-on sentence or comma splice error: two independent clauses joined only by a comma.

   Option B is incorrect because 'moreover' is an incorrect transition word indicating similarity with the preceding idea.

   Option D is incorrect 'inasmuch as' signifies a cause and effect relationship. Contextually it is illogical to infer that since some [proteins] can be purified from blood, it should not be expensive and not run a risk of contamination.

   The correct answer is C.

6. This is a question on grammatical construction.

   Let us bring out the sentence, "*Proteins can be produced in human cell culture but costs are very high and output small.*"

   Option D is the correct answer because it is devoid of any ambiguity. 'their', a possessive pronoun, correctly refers to 'proteins.'

   Option B is incorrect because 'its', a singular possessive pronoun, cannot refer to a plural subject, 'proteins.'

   Options A and C are incorrect because 'small output' could refer to the size of the final product; 'low' output refers to low productivity and is the appropriate adjective here.

   The correct answer is D.

7. This is a question on the usage of quantifiers.

   Let us bring out the related sentences, "*<u>Proteins can be produced in human cell culture but their costs are very high and output too low. Much larger quantities can be produced in bacteria or yeast but the proteins produced can be difficult to purify</u> and they lack the appropriate post-translational modifications that are needed for efficacy in vivo.*"

   Option A is the correct answer because 'Much' as a quantity word correct refers to uncountable noun, proteins; moreover, 'larger' is correct because a comparison is being made with the quantity of output mentioned in the preceding sentence.

   Option B is incorrect because a comparison is warranted with the low output mentioned in the preceding sentence and 'large' does not indicate the comparison.

Option C is incorrect because 'Many' as a quantity word is used for countable nouns, which is not the case here.

Option D is incorrect because 'too much quantities' does not indicate a comparison, but indicates excess.'

The correct answer is A.

8. This is a question on understanding tables and graphs.

   Let us bring out the sentence, *"The table shows that there are as many as three therapeutic proteins that can be used to cure cancer; however only two are commercially available."*

   Option A is the correct answer; refer to the third column of the table, exactly three therapeutic proteins–Thyroid stimulating hormones, TNF-alpha, and Trastuzumab–are meant to cure cancer; refer to the fourth column of the table, only two among these three–Thyroid stimulating hormones, and Trastuzumab– are commercially available.

   The correct answer is A.

9. This is a question on modifiers.

   Let us bring out the sentence, *"By contrast, human proteins have appropriate post-trans-lational modifications can be produced in the milk of transgenic sheep, goats and cattle."*

   Option B is the correct answer because the sentence in the current form is a run-on sentence and 'that' correctly modifies 'human proteins'.

   Option C is incorrect because 'which' because it is a non-restrictive clause and here the restrictive clause beginning with 'that' is required.

   Option D is incorrect because only a pair of commas or set-off commas (human proteins, having appropriate post-translational modifications, can) could make some sense here and there is only one comma, rendering the sentence meaningless.

   The correct answer is B.

10. This is a question on sentence construction.

    Let us bring out the sentence, *"Currently, research groups around the world are investigating whether these transgenic animals can be used to produce therapeutic proteins."*

    Option A is the correct answer because 'these' correctly refers to 'sheep, goats, cattle, pigs, rabbits and chickens', and the sentence is grammatically correct.

    Option B is incorrect because 'those' is an incorrect demonstrative pronoun to refer to'sheep, goats, cattle, pigs, rabbits and chickens' mentioned in sentence 1.

    Options C and D are incorrect because they lack concision and are wordy.

    The correct answer is A.

11. This is a question on organization of ideas.

    Let us bring out the related sentences, *"[1] By contrast, human proteins that have appro-priate post-translational modifications can be produced in the milk of transgenic sheep, goats, cattle, pigs, rabbits and chickens. [2] The animals are used as sterile bioreactors to produce large, complex proteins or proteins that can't be made in other cell systems. [3] Currently, research groups around the world are investigating whether these transgenic animals can be used to produce therapeutic proteins. [4] Output can be as high as 40 g per litre of milk and costs are relatively low."*

Option C is the correct answer because 'these' in sentence 3 needs an antecedent 'sheep, goats, cattle, pigs, rabbits and chickens'. Thus, sentence 3 should be placed after sentence 1; currently it is far away from the subject.

For above reason, other options are incorrect.

The correct answer is C.

Chapter 8

Speak to Us

Have a Question?

Please email your questions to info@manhattanreview.com. We will be happy to answer you. You questions can be related to a concept, an application of a concept, an explanation of a question, a suggestion for an alternate approach, or anything else you wish to ask regarding the SAT.

Please do mention the page number when quoting from the book.

Best of luck!

Manhattan Admissions

**You are a unique candidate with unique experience.
We help you to sell your story to the admissions committee.**

Manhattan Admissions is an educational consulting firm that guides academic candidates through the complex process of applying to the world's top educational programs. We work with applicants from around the world to ensure that they represent their personal advantages and strength well and get our clients admitted to the world's best business schools, graduate programs and colleges.

We will guide you through the whole admissions process:

- ☑ **Personal Assessment and School Selection**
- ☑ **Definition of your Application Strategy**
- ☑ **Help in Structuring your Application Essays**
- ☑ **Unlimited Rounds of Improvement**
- ☑ **Letter of Recommendation Advice**
- ☑ **Interview Preparation and Mock Sessions**
- ☑ **Scholarship Consulting**

To schedule a free 30-minute consulting and candidacy evaluation session or read more about our services, please visit or call:

 www.manhattanadmissions.com   **+1.212.334.2500**

Made in the USA
Lexington, KY
23 September 2016